As an Op...  the BA degree module *Childhood* for those wanting to work ... children. She has also privately tutored children aged ... eighteen in Maths, English and Science. She became ... terested in the power of nutrition to build children's ... and development progress and became aware that modern diet is not giving children what they need. As ... it she went on to qualify as a nutritionist and ran a ...onal therapy practice where she helped many people, ...ges, improve their health through better nutrition. ... also raised three children, she is very aware of the ... al challenges that parents face in getting their children ... well.

Other Titles

Can I Eat That? A nutritional guide through the dietary maze for type 2 diabetics

Delicious Gluten-Free Baking

Mediterranean Cooking for Diabetics

The Healthy Slow Cooker Cookbook

Stress-Free Feeding

The Olive Oil Diet

Bright Minds and Healthy Bodies

The best food and diet for your children's physical and intellectual health

HILDA GLICKMAN

ROBINSON

ROBINSON

First published in Great Britain 2017 by Robinson

1 3 5 7 9 10 8 6 4 2

Copyright © Hilda Glickman, 2017

The moral right of the author has been asserted.

A CIP catalogue record for this book
is available from the British Library.

Important note
This book is not intended as a substitute for medical advice or treatment.
Any person with a condition requiring medical attention should consult a
qualified medical practitioner or suitable therapist.

ISBN: 978-1-47213-783-8

Typeset in Bembo by Initial Typesetting Services, Edinburgh
Printed and bound in Great Britain by CPI Group (UK), Croydon CRO 4YY

Papers used by Robinson are from well-managed forests and
other responsible sources.

CONTENTS

Contents

Contents

Contents

Chapter 1

FOOD AND YOUR CHILD

We all want the best for our children. Giving them the most nutritious diet is one of the most important ways that we can influence their health, their intelligence and their behaviour. Food builds our bodies and our minds, and affects all aspects of our health and wellbeing. However, we need to eat the right food – the food that we have eaten for thousands of years, the food that we were meant to eat.

The problem is that much of what we eat today is dramatically different from what we ate in the past. It both lacks nutrients and is full of artificial additives and ingredients that were never heard of just a century ago. Much of it does very little for us or our families. But you can change this for your children. As they are still growing and have small stomachs, everything they eat should be the most nutritious you can give them. This book will show how to give them the very best start in life, not just for their bodies but also for their brains.

Food and your child's brain

Can your children concentrate well at school? Are they calm and focused or do they have temper tantrums? Some parents think that intelligence is genetic and that there is not much you can do to influence it after a child is born. Others believe that the environment plays a large part in how intelligent a child becomes and therefore try to influence it through stimulation with educational toys, games and books. The truth is that both genetics and the environment have an influence on a child's intelligence and wellbeing, and it is very difficult to separate them. But what our children eat is also tremendously important. The best nutrition can also affect how genes are expressed. It influences a child's environment in the womb and later: what a mother eats when pregnant, and even before conception, will affect the health of the child. The father's diet is also important up until conception.

What we eat affects our brains as much as our bodies. It is vital for brain health because, like the rest of our bodies, the brain is made from food – as are the chemical messengers that transmit signals throughout the brain. Although the idea that what we eat affects our brains is relatively new, the very latest research shows that this really is the case for children (as well as adults). The best food will help children do better at school, sleep well, concentrate better and think more clearly. Every aspect of thinking, from concentration to memory to intelligence, is affected by the food we eat.

In fact, the brain is as much as 60 per cent fat, and this nutrient is vital for all manner of cognitive ability. However, not any old fat will do; it has to be the right fat, the fat that we ate before food processing began. A study carried out by Dr Alex Richardson of the University of Oxford found that children who were given supplements of omega-3 and omega-6 essential fatty acids showed improvement in reading, spelling and behaviour within three months.[1] Omega-3 also has a positive effect on the oils in our skin, inflammation and our ability to heal. And these are just two nutrients out of the sixty or so that we need. Given on their own as supplements they are proven to help mental ability, but feeding your child the best diet that naturally supplies all the important nutrients is even better. This is what I recommend in this book.

Brains are constantly changing

Brain development and cognitive ability are not static. Our brain changes throughout childhood and does not stop developing until we reach our twenties. Even after that, the brain can change and regenerate to a degree. However, in order to develop properly it needs both the right stimulation and the right nutrients. Your child will not be as bright and capable as they could be if their diet is not good enough to feed the brain.

Building better brains and bodies

Every part of our bodies – hair, nails, bones, blood, hormones, even our genes – is made from nutrients, and these nutrients come from food. If our nutrition is not right, we will not be able to have the strongest bones, the healthiest blood, the smartest brain or the best immunity. All parts of the body need the full spectrum of nutrients. If some are lacking, this will affect the whole system, because nutrients act in synergy with each other. For example, most people know that bones need calcium, but it actually takes very many different vitamins and minerals to make bone, including calcium, magnesium, boron, phosphorus, strontium, vitamin K and vitamin D, and all of these nutrients need to be in balance. If we eat lots of dairy food but no leafy green vegetables we might take too much calcium, which would cause a deficiency of magnesium. This is why just taking high doses of one nutrient in a supplement is not a good idea.

Our diet is only as good as the weakest link in the chain. However, the typical diet that children are eating today is not conducive to healthy brain or physical development. However, if we change our children's diets we can go a long way towards helping them grow the best brains and the best and healthiest bodies possible. This book will show you how to choose the best foods for your children and how to incorporate them into your family's life in a pleasant and simple way.

Different interests

The main aim of food manufacturers is to sell food. They try to produce food that is tasty and tempting for the consumer, but unfortunately the health aspect often takes a back seat. Legally food does not have to be healthy – it has to be safe, but this is a different thing. Being safe means that it cannot make you ill in the short term by containing dangerous bacteria or being rotten or downright poisonous. But, even if food is not unsafe in the short term, that doesn't mean it is particularly healthy; and if it is low in nutrients and high in artificial chemicals, sugar and the wrong type of fat, it may make you ill in the long term.

One reason for misinformation is that leaflets on healthy eating are often produced by the food companies themselves, which means that processed cereals and sweetened drinks may be advertised as 'healthy'.

Journalists seem to be forever writing about 'healthy eating', but they do not always get it right – they are not trained nutritionists, so may just rely on simple ideas that they have read somewhere else. Also, research into nutrition is being carried out all the time, but we usually only get to hear about a small number of all the studies that are published – and these are often the strange or unusual. Newspapers or magazines need the different and the dramatic in order to sell more copies. There is no official body that aims to tell the public the truth about food.

How to use this book

This book will tell you the truth about what to eat and what to feed your children. I do not have any vested interests. My aim is to report the most recent and best information about healthy eating in the clearest and most practical way.

The next few chapters are all about what your child should be eating and why. Chapters 5 and 6 give lots of quick and easy examples of foods and meals they can eat every day. Chapters 8 to 10 look in more detail at the problems with many of the foods that we are encouraged to give our children, from children's menus to low-fat diets. The last few chapters give advice on different problems and issues, from how to handle children's parties to managing as your children get older, and the chemicals in our homes.

Not just for children

This book is about the best food for your child's growth and development. However, the advice given is not just for children. The good news is that if you as parents adopt the same way of eating, you should also be healthier. It is a diet that will help your brain remain healthy as you age. Not surprisingly, it is also the diet that will help your children in turn produce healthy children themselves. We need the right nutrients in the correct amount for all aspects of our health – to build our brain and bodies, to help them function properly and to prevent future illness.

In a nutshell

- Feeding children the best food is essential for their healthy growth and development.

- As children are still growing and have small stomachs, everything they eat should be the best that you can give them.

- Children's brains, like the rest of their bodies, are made from nutrients that come from food. The best food will help them do better at school, sleep well, concentrate better and think more clearly.

- Very many of the foods sold in the shops are highly processed, lacking in nutrients and not doing our children any good.

- There is a great deal of confusion about food, because much food information is produced and distributed by those with vested interests.

- Adults also need the best food, and the advice given in this book should help parents to reduce the likelihood of succumbing to many diseases.

Chapter 2

GENERAL AIMS FOR FEEDING YOUR CHILD

What should we feed our children? The answer is really quite simple. We should eat the food that we have survived on for thousands of years. This means food that is fresh, natural and as close to its original state as possible. Ideally, it should not have been processed in any way and should retain the nutrients that nature gave it. This means that an apple is better than apple juice or apple pie, a piece of fresh fish is better than fish paste or highly battered fish fingers, and fresh organic grass-fed meat is infinitely better than sausages, ham, bacon or other processed meats. The food we eat should also retain its natural colours and flavours and not be coloured or flavoured with artificial chemical additives.

With all the different foods on offer, how do you decide whether something is good for you or your children? A simple way is to think about where it came from. Was it made by nature or manufactured in a factory? When I give talks on healthy eating, I often ask my audience what they would eat if stranded on a deserted island. They usually say 'coconuts' because that is what immediately springs to mind. However, I would hope our island would be rather more fertile than that. After giving it a bit more thought they usually say things like fruit, vegetables, fish, meat, nuts and seeds, all grown organically, picked ripe and not stored for long periods of time. They are the things that we used to eat in their natural state and this is how we should all be eating today. There would be no pot noodles, pasta, sugary foods (except for natural sugars found in fruit), crisps or breakfast cereals. These are made in factories and are very different from the natural food on which our species developed, and which we still need today.

We can try our best

Nowadays we can't, of course, eat completely natural food, as we have little choice but to buy what is in the shops. However, buying natural food fresh and cooking it ourselves should be our ideal aim. The bulk of our diet should be made up of healthy, unadulterated, unprocessed foods cooked in a simple way or left raw, as in the case of fruit or vegetables like avocados or watercress. These are the foods that we survived on for most of our history. They contain the highest concentration of nutrients that will help your children grow and develop at their best.

Some foods may seem natural and healthy because we are

so used to eating them: bread, breakfast cereals, pasta and 'healthy whole grains'. However, these foods are very new additions to our diet. Grains only came into our lives in the last 10,000 years or so. In addition to this, the last fifty years or so has seen such huge changes in the way that food is produced that many items would be unrecognisable to our great-grandparents.

Not everything in food has been identified

Natural foods are not simple. They contain literally thousands of chemicals and nutrients, and more are being discovered all the time. Although we know about quite a few of them, we still do not know all of nature's secrets. For example, around four hundred different chemicals have been identified in garlic, but there are probably more. Thousands of new chemicals have been found in fruits and vegetables in the last few decades. In the recent past, it was thought that foods contained just protein, fats, carbohydrates, vitamins and minerals. It is now known that there is a staggering amount of protective chemicals in natural unprocessed foods. They are found mainly in the colour pigments and the odours and flavours of fruit and vegetables, so if we eat plenty of these we stand a good chance of ingesting both known nutrients and those not yet discovered. For example, the red pigment in carrots contains beta-carotene, an antioxidant that neutralises dangerous free radicals which cause all sorts of health issues; the yellow pigment in corn contains lutein and zeaxanthin, which can help prevent us getting eye problems such as cataracts and macular degeneration.

Processed foods, or foods which have been changed dramatically from their original state, will give us few if any of these important chemicals. White bread and pasta are very poor foods, devoid of many nutrients and containing no phytochemicals, but today we eat so much more bread and cereal-based foods than fruit and vegetables.

Eat a rainbow diet

We should eat natural foods to get the benefits of all the antioxidants and phytochemicals contained in them. Many of these come from the thousands of coloured pigments found in fruit and vegetables – the red and orange colours in strawberries, oranges, raspberries and cherries and the blue/black pigments in prunes, blueberries and blackberries – so it is very important that we eat a colourful diet in order to get all the phytochemicals that we need. Natural flavours, too, contain powerful plant chemicals that positively affect our health.

However, we have been too clever. We have managed to make these flavours and colours artificially, and then put them into all sorts of food, including sweets, yogurts, cakes, desserts and confectionary. Therefore, instead of getting the amazingly valuable properties of the plant chemicals in natural food, we get the synthetic flavours and colours made in a laboratory that have none of these. For example, the flavour and colour in a strawberry yoghurt is often artificial. They do not give us the wonderful properties of the real colour pigment – and might even be harmful.

Artificial colours and flavours are not just deficient – they can also be harmful. An article published in the French journal *Prescrire International* carried out a study where 297 children representative of the general population were given a diet without food colourings, followed by a diet containing food colourings. The results showed that when the children ate the diet containing the colourings they became more hyperactive.[1]

It annoys me so much that we are expected to eat artificially coloured and flavoured foods. Many people do not realise that the flavours and colours are not made from real food, and so lack all the protective properties real food supplies. But the lesson is: if you want strawberry yogurt – add real strawberries.

We need a wide variety of foods

We are now able to eat the same foods repeatedly, and studies have shown that most of us do. We tend to stick to the few foods that we like, and as a result many children's diets have become very limited. This then limits the number of nutrients taken in, as different foods contain different things so we are not getting everything that we need. In the past we were forced to eat different foods throughout the year as not everything was in season all the time. If we liked apples, for example, we would have had to wait until the autumn when they were ripe. Before then, we would have had to eat whatever other foods were ready to eat. Now we can eat any type of fruit and vegetable all year round.

This is good in one way: children who only likes peas can eat them all year round. But still, try to give your children all sorts of different foods so that they get the widest variety of vitamins, minerals and other nutrients.

Healthy eating should be easy

Simple home-cooked natural foods are the best foods to give your children. Meals containing fresh meat, chicken and fish together with lots of vegetables have sustained us well for many years. Not everyone feels confident about cooking everything fresh, but it is not difficult.

Do you worry about your cooking skills? Do you ever feel pressurised to make meals from fancy recipes? It's easy to be intimidated by celebrity cooks, and those TV programmes that judge contestants on their cooking skills. We seem to have become a nation that loves to watch people cooking and preparing all sorts of elaborate and delicious dishes, and any bookshop assistant will tell you that recipe books by famous cooks sell more than any other kind.

But at the same time, the supermarkets are full of ready

meals and our high streets full of takeaways. Studies have shown that we actually cook very little ourselves. In fact, we are cooking less than previous generations, and many people can't cook at all. It seems that while many people like watching cookery programmes on TV, they can make us feel inadequate if we're not able to rustle up a fancy three-course meal when we get in from work. For those new to cooking, it can make the subject look more complicated than it is.

But don't worry. Your children do not need difficult or complicated recipes with lots of different and unusual ingredients. You can feed your children very well with the minimum of complicated cooking, such as following wonderfully healthy meals:

• Fresh, simmered ordinary vegetables

• Baked meat

• Plain chicken roasted in coconut oil

• Casseroles and stews

• Potatoes baked in the oven

• Scrambled eggs

• Fresh soups

• Fresh fruit

These simply prepared foods are more nutritious than more elaborate and complicated dishes. It doesn't have to take much time either. Often it is easier and quicker to make your own than buy microwave dishes (and it is certainly cheaper).

Mealtimes should be happy times

Feeding children well is not always easy. We all want our children to eat well, and healthy eating is certainly about getting your children to ingest the most nutritious foods. However, eating is not just about the physical act of putting food into your mouth. Food is a very emotive subject. It is part of our whole culture – our emotions, our feelings and even our personalities are involved.

Do you associate different types of food with different people? As a child, did you always have a certain type of food when visiting a specific relative? Does that particular food fondly remind you of that person? On the other hand, were you forced to eat food you did not like? And has this coloured your attitude to that food forever?

Eating meals containing good healthy food should be associated with happy times, and not problems and arguments. Keeping mealtimes pleasant is important, as this affects digestion and absorption, and later on it will affect attitudes to food. I know that this is not always easy to achieve.

However, it is very easy for me just to say this – making it happen is another story! Some children are very fussy eaters, and mealtimes can become a source of great frustration for parents. If your children are used to a diet with plenty of 'children's' processed foods, they may not be happy about the change to freshly prepared, home-cooked meals. It is very hard to stay relaxed when all you want is to give your children the very best, but you are thwarted at every turn.

Sometimes the less said about the food the better. Just put it in front of them and don't make a fuss. Give a sense that 'this is what we eat in this family'. Eating with your children helps. Even if you are going to have your proper meal later, you can make up a small plate for yourself and join your children as they eat their meal. This will show them that they aren't different – that they should be eating the same sort of foods as you.

If your child hates a particular food, don't try to force it. This will only lead to temper tantrums. Instead, say very little and then try to introduce it again a few months later.

Children like familiarity and routine. If you begin giving them the type of food you want them to eat when young, that is what they will expect to eat – and enjoy – later on.

If you bring up your children on the diet described in this book, they will get used to the taste of good, fresh food, and prefer it to the artificially flavoured, additive-enhanced junk food sold all around us.

In addition to eating a wide variety of natural foods, there are two other main factors to consider when feeding your children. The first is to make sure they are getting enough of the good fats: the fats which help build our brains and bodies, and keep them functioning. The second is to keep their blood sugar balanced, so that their energy is balanced throughout the day, which aids concentration (and prevents mood swings!). The next two chapters look at these in turn.

In a nutshell

- We should try to eat the type of food that we have survived on for most of our history.

- Natural foods contain thousands of chemicals and nutrients, and more are being discovered all the time.

- We should eat a rainbow of vegetables and fruit, as many different nutrients are found in natural colour pigments.

- We also need to eat a variety of different foods to get all the important nutrients that we need.

- Artificially coloured and flavoured foods do not have these natural nutrients.

- Healthy home-cooked food can be very easy to prepare.

- Mealtimes should be happy times, to help digestion and to build good associations with healthy food.

- If your child doesn't like a certain food, say little about it and try reintroducing it later.

Chapter 3

THE RIGHT FATS

Fats are one of the most important elements of our diet, but we are bombarded with so much conflicting advice and false information about them. Many people who want to lose weight are encouraged to steer away from the natural fats in meat towards unhealthy, processed and damaged fats. But fats are vital for the health of ourselves and our children and they perform many important functions in our bodies. They are especially important for your children's brains.

So often, we hear that fats cause heart disease and make you fat, but this is not the case. We need to eat fat. In fact, we need fats so much that some are called 'essential fatty acids'. These are fats we cannot make in our bodies and so we need to eat foods that contain them. There are other types of fat we also need, so don't be afraid of fats and make sure that your child's diet is not deficient.

Fats in our diet can be divided into saturated fat that comes from foods like meat, cheese, butter; unsaturated fat that comes from fish, nuts and seeds; and monounsaturated fat from olive oil. But, having said that, many foods contain a mixture of different types of fat.

Why we need fats

We are made up of millions of cells and each cell has a membrane surrounding it. This membrane protects the cell from harmful substances, controlling what goes in. The membrane is made from fat: omega-3 from the chemicals EPA and DHA found in oily fish and omega-6 from alpha-linolenic acid, which is found in nuts and seeds.

However, your body will construct the membrane from any fat that it can find. Many adults and children are consuming so much processed oil that this is going into their cell membranes, stopping them from functioning as well as they should. They become rigid and don't protect our cells properly.

Fats and the brain

So, good fats can help our children's brain development and keep it functioning well. A deficiency of good fats is associated with all sorts of problems related to memory and learning, mood and behaviour, as well as much physical illness such as heart disease and cancer.

Omega-3 and omega-6: the essential oils that nature gave us

There are two types of fat that are essential but can't be made in our bodies. These are omega-3 and omega-6. Omega-3 comes from oily fish like salmon, sardines and herring, and omega-6 comes from nuts (e.g. walnuts), seeds (e.g. sesame, sunflower and pumpkin) and wheat germ. Before food processing became widespread, these foods would have been our only source of the oils. Actually there would have been no pressed oil at all. Now we consume vast quantities of oils squeezed out from these foods, but these oils are so heavily processed that they are as nothing found in nature. I discuss this more below.

Are we getting enough?

Our intake of oily fish has decreased dramatically during the last hundred years and the ratio of omega-3 to omega-6 has changed. Now we eat far more omega-6 than ever before. In Europe and the United States there are high levels of omega-6 and low levels of omega-3 in our diets. It is thought that we evolved on a ratio of 1:1, but now in the West we ingest about twenty times more omega-6 than omega-3.

Another problem is that the omega-6 we are eating is not good, coming from these processed oils like sunflower, corn and rapeseed/canola. Processing changes the oil dramatically.

Signs your child is low in omega-3

- Dry skin
- Dry scaly rash
- Dry eyes
- Cracked nails
- Poor wound healing
- Rough bumpy skin on the outside of the upper arms

These are the signs that are easy to spot. However, low levels affect your child's body in less obvious ways, as omega-3 is related to inflammation. Inflammation can damage artery walls, and cholesterol attaches to them as part of the repair mechanism. If there is too much cholesterol, the arteries block. One study published in the journal *PLos One* looked at 493 healthy school children aged seven to nine from mainstream schools. They found that 'concentrations of DHA and other Omega-3 [fats] . . . were low' relative to those recommended for adult healthy hearts.[1]

Sources of essential fatty acids

Omega-3

Salmon

Sardines

Herring

Anchovies

Mackerel

Flaxseeds and hempseeds

Walnuts

Omega-6

Most nuts

Hempseeds

Flaxseeds

Sesame seeds

Soya beans

Wheat germ

Sources of other good fats

Omega-9

Olive oil

Saturated fat

Coconut oil

Cream

Butter

Meat fat

Cheese

These are all the fats we should be eating, and they have been in our diets since the beginning of time.

However, very new man-made oils have been added to our diets and these are now found everywhere in the food chain. They take the place of the fats that we should be eating and are damaging for you and your children.

Easy ways with fish

Here are some ideas to get more fish into your diet:

- Add chopped organic salmon to pizzas along with more vegetables.

- Mix pieces of fish with rice and vegetables for an interesting risotto.

- Try pickled herring, chopped herring or rollmops.

- Make fishcakes with cooked salmon and cooked mashed potato. Add these together and form into cakes.

- Fish tinned in spring water can be used if in a hurry. Do not use fish tinned in oil or tomato sauce as these are processed. If you can only get the kind tinned in brine (salty water), wash off the brine.

- Try fish pie made with cod or haddock, mushrooms and mashed potato.

- Sweet and sour herring is a tasty, interesting dish.

- Place some chopped onion with some vinegar and a little honey on a fish fillet, take one end and roll it up. Secure with a cocktail stick. Bake in the oven.

Omega-3 for vegetarians

If you hate fish or are vegetarian, you can still get omega-3 by eating flaxseeds and walnuts. However, these do not deliver the same benefits as eating fish. This is because the oil in these has to be converted to the DHA and EPA found naturally in oily fish. Some people's bodies are not good at making this conversion, but if you are vegetarian it is worth eating these seeds and nuts.

Olive oil

This type of oil has become very popular in recent years. It is not one of the essential fats like fish oil or omega-6, but it is quite nutritious and contains omega-9, among other fatty acids. Supermarkets are full of different varieties from all over Europe, but, some are more processed than others. Always buy extra virgin olive oil as this is the nearest to oil in its natural state.

If used for cooking, olive oil should not be allowed to smoke. It is better not to use it for cooking at all, but instead use it on salads as they do in Mediterranean countries.

Coconut oil

Coconut oil is useful as it is more stable than vegetable oil, so it does not go off. The oil occurs naturally in the coconut, so is minimally processed. It can be used for cooking as it is not easily oxidised in heat.

In a nutshell

- Eating the right fats is very important for your child's health.

- The essential fatty acids are omega-3 from oily fish and omega-6 from nuts and seeds. Most people don't eat enough omega-3.

- Vegetarians can get omega-3 from flaxseeds and walnuts, but it is not exactly the same as fish.

- The only oil you should buy is extra virgin olive oil, but this shouldn't be used for cooking.

Chapter 4

BALANCING YOUR CHILD'S
BLOOD SUGAR

Do your children get upset and irritable if they have not eaten for a few hours? Do they have temper tantrums if they miss a meal or dinner is late? Do they find it hard to concentrate on what they are doing if they have not eaten for a while? Many children have these issues, and often it is due the fact that their blood sugar has dropped too low. Low blood sugar, or hypoglycaemia, is not an illness, but a very common condition that affects many children and adults. It is also called reactive hypoglycaemia because it is really a reaction to the type of food eaten a few hours earlier.

People suffering from diabetes can have spells of low blood sugar, but I am not referring to this here. Many children and adults who are not diabetic also have trouble balancing their blood sugar, and this is mainly due to the modem way of eating.

Reactive hypoglycaemia is caused by ingesting large amounts of sugar and simple carbohydrates. This means white bread, pasta, cakes, biscuits, processed cereals like corn flakes and coco pops, without the help of protein or fat. When children eat these high carbohydrate foods, their blood sugar rises too high too quickly. If you plotted their sugar levels on a graph, you would see a very sharp rise or spike. In order to help it travel into the cells, insulin is produced, but this has the effect of causing the sugar in the blood to drop.

The more sugar that is eaten the more insulin is produced, and the more the blood sugar will drop a few hours later. This drop in blood sugar gives rise to some of the symptoms listed below.

Adults and children with this problem will then reach for another cake or biscuit or other sugary snack, and the whole process begins again – the blood sugar rises very high only to drop a few hours later. The rise and fall of blood sugar throughout the day becomes like a roller coaster, when what we really want is to keep it relatively stable. It should drop a little before meals and rise a little after meals, but it should not rise too high and then drop very low.

Symptoms of low blood sugar

- Dizziness
- Hunger
- Shakiness

- Feeling light-headed

- Confused or foggy thinking

- Nervousness

- Irritability

- Crying spells

- Temper tantrums

- Tiredness

- Poor concentration

- Disturbed sleep

- Inability to sit still

Children may show just a few of these symptoms, and of course the symptoms can be caused by other conditions as well (do check with your doctor if you have concerns). But this demonstrates how important it is to keep your child's blood sugar as stable as possible throughout the whole day. This can be done quite easily with the right diet.

How to keep blood sugar stable

In order to keep their blood sugar stable children (and adults) need to have good quality meals and snacks at regular intervals. Every meal, no matter how small, needs to consist of some protein, carbohydrate and fat.

Protein and fat are digested much more slowly than the carbohydrate, and so stop our blood sugar rising too high too quickly. We want our blood sugar to rise slowly after a meal, and for the sugar or glucose to drip into our bloodstream slowly throughout the next few hours. This is what happens when your child eats a proper meal. On the other hand, eating sweets or refined carbohydrates on their own will cause a sharp spike in blood sugar and your child will pay the price later by having crying spells or temper tantrums.

One of the most important ways to make sure that blood sugar remains stable is to have a good breakfast, and in Chapter 6 I suggest breakfasts that contain protein, carbohydrate and fat, while still being quite simple to prepare. Your child's food throughout the day should also have these three elements.

Protein foods

The highest amount of protein is found in foods derived from animals.

- Meat, preferably organic
- Chicken, organic
- Organic free-range eggs
- Fish
- Cheese
- Yogurt

Other sources of protein with lesser amounts

- Nuts and seeds

- Quinoa

- Peas, beans and lentils mixed together to include all the amino acids

Carbohydrate foods

We often think of carbohydrate foods as bread, cakes, biscuits, pasta, rice and potatoes, but these are not the only foods that are mainly carbohydrates. Food charts show these in a category of their own and label them as carbohydrates, but this is misleading, as vegetables and fruits are carbohydrates too. Some contain more than others, but they are nearly all carbohydrate, containing almost no fat or protein. Salad vegetables contain less, but 'starchy' vegetables such as carrots, swede, parsnips and potatoes contain much more.

Starch is carbohydrate, and this is converted to sugar in the body quite quickly. If you think about it, you will realise that vegetables contain no fat and very little protein so they are mainly carbohydrate. For example, an average banana has 23g carbohydrate but only 1.1g protein and 0.3g fat, so it is a high-carbohydrate food.

However, fruit and vegetables are often seen as being in a different category from carbohydrates like bread and rice, and are often put into a separate section in charts. This is wrong. They are carbohydrate foods and very much better for us than refined sugar and wheat-based foods. Any food that tastes sweet contains carbohydrate.

- Sweet potatoes
- White potatoes
- Carrots
- Corn
- Parsnips
- Rice (use brown)
- Breads
- Oats
- All fresh fruits
- Dried fruits
- Bananas

Fats

Fats have had a bad press, but as discussed in Chapter 3 they are just as important as any other nutrient and are vital for health. The best fats are those listed below. Children need to eat some fat at every meal in order to keep their blood sugar stable.

- The natural fat in oily fish
- The fat in nuts and seeds

- Extra virgin olive oil

- Fresh organic butter

- Nut butters (also contain protein)

- Coconut oil for cooking

- The natural fat in good quality organic meat

Vitamins and minerals

All nutrients are dependent on each other, so for stable blood sugar you also need to consider vitamins, minerals and other nutrients. They are found in most unprocessed foods, so if you stick to fresh fruits, vegetables, meat, fish, nuts, seeds and yogurt you should be able to get these. Of course, it still depends on the quality of the soil in which they were grown.

Avoid sugary foods

Eating cakes, biscuits, sweets and other sugary foods causes low blood sugar, so either cut these out or keep them down to a minimum. If children do want something sweet, it should be with a meal rather than on its own. Snacks should not be sugary unless accompanied by some protein and fat.

We can try our best. Of course, you cannot always control what they eat when others are looking after them, particularly at parties (which we look at in more detail in Chapter 12), but you can let other adults know your concerns. You can also keep sweet processed foods out of your house.

The lists of meals and snacks described in the next two chapters give suggestions that will help. There will always be a protein food together with a carbohydrate food and some fat. This is the formula you should stick to for keeping your child's blood sugar stable.

In a nutshell

- One of the most important things we can do for our children is to make sure that their blood sugar is balanced.

- Low blood sugar can result in crying spells, irritability, inability to concentrate, temper tantrums, fatigue and more.

- To balance blood sugar, your children need to have regular meals consisting of protein, fat and carbohydrate.

- A good quality breakfast with these ratios is also very important.

- Sweet sugary foods should not be eaten, but if they are, they should only come after a meal or with some protein food.

- Regular snacks following the rules can help stabilise blood sugar.

Chapter 5

VERY EASY QUICK NATURAL FOODS

For a busy family, quick easy food is often the priority. The good news is that many natural, healthy foods contain the most nutrients when eaten raw or are simply prepared. This chapter lists some of the best foods for your children. If they need cooking at all they can quickly and easily be simmered or made into a casserole. In fact they are just as easy to prepare as microwaved ready meals. I hope that you will enjoy feeding your children in this way and love eating these foods yourself.

Eggs

Eggs are very high in nutrients and very easy to digest. They contain B vitamins, good quality protein and the minerals selenium, magnesium, iodine and zinc. They contain very important fats called phospholipids, which are needed throughout the body and particularly in the brain. They are also rich in choline, which is needed to make acetylcholine, which the brain uses for learning and other cognitive processes.

We all know that eggs have been maligned because of the cholesterol connection, but the latest thinking is that cholesterol does not cause heart disease. It is needed in every cell of the body and has many functions, including in the production of vitamin D. In fact, 85 per cent of cholesterol is produced in the body and does not come from what we eat.

Eggs are easy and quick to prepare. It takes just a few minutes to rustle up a scrambled or boiled egg, and these are very easy for children to digest.

Avoid frying eggs, as this can destroy the essential fats and phospholipids. However, if a little fat is used make sure it is butter or coconut oil. Remember that eggs should be cooked. Raw eggs in any food should not be eaten, and especially not given to children.

The best eggs

I recommend that you buy organic free-range eggs. (All organic eggs are free range but not all free-range eggs are organic.) Organically fed chickens are better because they are fed food that is more nutritious, are not given antibiotics and are exposed to the sun and fresh air. The quality of an egg depends on what the chickens are fed and so you should go for the best you can afford. There are also omega-3 eggs where the chickens have been fed a diet that contains seeds high in this nutrient.

Fish

The oils in fish are so important for our bodies and brains, as discussed in Chapter 3. Salmon, sardines and other oily fish are high in omega-3, which is essential for good brain development and function. However, many children do not like fish and it is not always easy to dream up interesting ways of serving it. Here are some ideas:

- Make a risotto with pieces of salmon, brown rice, peas and chopped cooked carrots.

- Add fish to home-made pizza with thin dough and some vegetables.

- Make chopped herring (see overleaf).

- Try sweet and sour herring.

- Make fish cakes with mashed cooked salmon blended with mashed potato and shaped into cakes.

- Use in open sandwiches made with baby rolls.

Salmon

Salmon is high in omega-3 fats. It is very easy to prepare and can be poached or baked in the oven. If you decide to bake it, try not to use much fat as this will compete with the omega-3. It is also not a good idea to fry it.

There is some controversy about farmed salmon. If they are fed on cereals rather than the small fish (plankton) that they are supposed to eat, the salmon will not contain the same amount of omega-3 fast as wild salmon. This is why I recommend buying wild salmon if you can. A similar food is trout, which is a good alternative. Smoked salmon is not good for children as it is too high in salt.

Chopped herring

This is an easy way to add oily fish to your children's diet, although it is probably best for older children as it's quite tart. Choose a jar that is sugar free and does not contain added vegetable oil. Some supermarkets stock it prepared, but this can taste a little sour – it is quite easy to make yourself. Rinse the herring very thoroughly before chopping, as it can be quite high in vinegar. Chop or mash it, then mash in hard-boiled eggs to taste. It can be used a delicious spread on rice cakes or good bread.

Tinned fish

Although it is better to eat fresh fish, tinned fish can sometimes be used when in a hurry. Sardines are valuable but buy them tinned in water, not brine (salty water) or oil. The oil is not good because it is processed oil, not from the fish, and will compete with the fish's natural omega-3. Tinned salmon can also be used but it is too salty for very young children. In any case, you should wash off the added salt as much as possible – not always easy, I know. I don't recommend tinned tuna as it is higher in mercury and not as rich in omega-3.

Vegetables

Vegetables should be the kingpins of everyone's diet. These contain the highest concentration of nutrients apart from meat, fish and eggs. They are high in vitamins, minerals and in particular phytochemicals, which help to protect us from all sorts of illnesses such as cancer, heart disease and Alzheimer's. Protein foods are acidic, and they need to be balanced with the alkalinity of vegetables. All vegetables are valuable, so try to give your children a wide variety. Both raw and cooked vegetables are good, so have both salads and cooked vegetables every day.

You can see that I am not saying 'fruits and vegetables'. This is because these are not the same and should not be lumped together (even though they always seem to be). Fruits are important, but not as important as vegetables. All of us should have some fruit and/or vegetables at every meal even breakfast. The government urges us to eat five portions a day but this is not enough. Ten portions a day is a good figure to aim for.

People often tell me that they eat 'lots of vegetables' but when I probe further they say that they eat something like peas and carrots with their evening meal and maybe a sliver of tomato in their lunchtime sandwiches. This is very little. Vegetables should form the main part of our diet.

Children need a variety of different vegetables, including root vegetables like swede, carrots and sweet potatoes. Potatoes are fine, but buy organic as non-organic potatoes are heavily sprayed with chemicals.

Ideas for using vegetables

- Make vegetable soup (see below).

- Add lots of vegetables to stews, spaghetti bolognaise and other meat dishes such as chilli con carne.

- Add to thin pizza bases.

- Make a pizza crust with mashed cauliflower.

- Blend extra vegetables into tomato sauce used for meat or other dishes.

- Add grated carrot and lots of salad vegetables to sandwiches.

- Add onions, tomatoes and mushrooms (cooked) to scrambled eggs.

- Try making vegetable noodles with a spiraliser which grinds vegetables into spiral shapes. They look like ordinary noodles but are healthier than wheat-based ones.

- Mash together cooked cabbage and potato to make the delicious Irish dish colcannon.

- Potatoes can be mashed with carrots and sweet potato for better value.

- Add vegetables to minced meat to create natural organic hamburgers.

- Make colourful vegetable kebabs by alternating cooked carrots, avocado and cooked swede on sticks.

- Mix lots of vegetables with rice and fish to make a healthy paella or biryani.

- Add cauliflower blended into soups as a thickener.

- Give children small stalks of celery with nut butter in the groove.

- Try sprouting mung beans and add to salads and sandwiches. Children can help with the sprouting.

- Add cress to mashed egg in sandwiches.

Soup is special

Homemade soups are one of the best foods you can give your children. If they are made correctly, they are full of vitamins, minerals and antioxidants, and are filling and warming in the winter. I am talking here about soups that contain a mixture of different vegetables rather than just one or two. This is a very good way to get your children to ingest many vegetables at once. It also saves you the bother of having one pot for carrots, another for cabbage and so on. The beauty of soups is that they are so easy to make and can be frozen in little containers for later use.

You may have been put off making soup, thinking that it requires all sorts of fancy recipes or time-consuming procedures. But soup is really easy. I use carrots, onions, swede, celery or any other vegetables I have around, simmer them until soft, and then use a stick blender that you put directly into the pan. Stick blenders are cheap to buy and easy to clean.

Don't worry too much about how much of each vegetable to include. With experience, you will find out what you like best. You can add other flavours for different soups. For minestrone, you can add some tomato purée or tinned tomatoes. If you boil up some chicken pieces (with the bone, but remove it before blending!), this will give a nice chicken soup.

In the old days, cooks used to make a roux, where butter and flour are blended together as a thickener. These ingredients are added to shop-bought soups to increase the thickness more cheaply. But you do not need to do this – it makes the soup less nutritious and gives it what I consider an unpleasant floury texture. A homemade soup with more vegetables and no flour is much better. If you want a thicker soup, add more vegetables and less water. Potatoes mashed into the soup or red split lentils are nutritious thickeners.

The best kind of soup

Adults often feel that we need to make what I call 'named soups', like carrot and coriander, or broccoli and Stilton, or French onion. If you feel like making a named soup, that is fine for adults, but a mixed vegetable soup is more nutritious and children do not need the sophistication of a title. For different flavours, you can add turmeric, tomato purée or curry powder. Don't forget cinnamon – this spice is often used in Middle Eastern cuisine, in meat dishes and in the delightful soup, harira.

Use real stock rather using a cube, which is full of chemicals. The flavour is wonderful! To make, get some organic chicken pieces or a whole chicken and boil for two or three hours. Meat bones are also good for giving a different flavour. You can add a few vegetables to make the stock extra tasty. After it has cooled, freeze it in small cartons and use it as stock whenever you make soup, adding lots more vegetables. Stock not only increases the nutrient content substantially but also makes the flavour much stronger and richer. For vegetarian stock, just don't use meat.

Bone broths are made from stock where the bones have been boiled at length. They contain collagen from the bones and glutamine, which repairs the gut lining, so are particularly good for anyone with digestive problems.

As with all the recommended foods in this book, vegetables soups are wonderful for adults too. They are so rich in antioxidants that they help prevent all sorts of diseases related to oxidation.

Casseroles and stews

Like soups, casseroles and stews are very nutritious because they contain a mixture of different foods in one bowl which help us ingest many nutrients. They also combine protein, fat and carbohydrate so keep children's blood sugar even, and are easy to eat and welcoming and tasty on cold winter days.

They are very easy to make, because you just put everything into the same pot and either simmer on the hob or cook in the oven. In some ways, oven cooking is better for those with young children, as you do not need to keep checking it all the time. Just put the casserole in the oven and leave it to cook. Any meat such as beef or chicken can be used and add carrots, courgettes, onions, swede, potatoes, in fact any vegetables that your child likes. If you are at work all day, a slow cooker could come in handy – simply throw in the ingredients before you leave for work, and it will cook slowly throughout the day.

Hummus

This is a very nutritious food but nearly every variety sold in shops contains rapeseed or sunflower oil, even those that mention olive oil in the ingredients, so be careful to read the labels. It is better to make your own. Blend a tin of chickpeas (rinse the salt off first) with some sesame seeds and lemon juice for a quick and nutritious hummus without processed oils. Chickpeas are nutritious, with both protein and carbohydrate. Sesame seeds are extremely rich in calcium and essential fatty acids, so they are good for people who cannot tolerate milk. Homemade hummus (without processed oil) is very useful in packed lunches and can be spread on rice cakes or good quality bread. However, like all foods high in oil, it should be kept in an airtight container in the fridge.

Small jacket potatoes

Jacket potatoes are so easy to make and a good source of natural carbohydrate. Just pop them in the oven, perhaps covered in foil, and bake until soft. The large jacket potatoes which are often served in snack bars and cafés contain too much starch – especially for younger children – which will raise blood sugar too high too quickly (see Chapter 4). Small potatoes bake just as well and take much less time. Potatoes should be served with protein such as chicken, so that your child's blood sugar remains stable. It is much better to buy organic potatoes, as non-organic ones are often heavily sprayed with pesticides.

Many cafés and restaurants sell jacket potatoes with tuna, where the tuna is loaded with mayonnaise. In fact, often there seems to be more mayonnaise than tuna! Do not touch this. Mayonnaise contains highly processed oil and will do your children no good at all.

Sweet potatoes

These are not really potatoes at all but are part of a family with the lovely name of morning glory. They are higher in nutrients, especially antioxidants, than ordinary potatoes – and children like them! Although they taste quite sweet, they don't tend to raise blood sugar as much as white potatoes. They can be boiled or baked in the oven or added to soups and stews. For baking just wrap in foil and put them in the oven.

Fruit

What could be easier to prepare and more natural than fresh fruit? I know this is obvious but sometimes fruit is forgotten. Clients who come to me for help have told me that they often just don't think about fruit. So how can you incorporate more fruit into your children's diets? One way is to leave a small bowl of washed fruits in the fridge, and let your children eat from it at will. Include cherry tomatoes and small stalks of celery.

Berries are especially good for children and adults as they contain very high levels of antioxidants, which protect us from free radicals – dangerous chemicals which cause all sorts of conditions from cataracts to cancer. Free radicals come from the environment, from factory pollution, cigarette smoke (millions per puff), radiation from the sun, and even from the metabolic processes that go on in our own bodies. Antioxidants help to neutralise free radicals, and the highest amount of antioxidants are contained in the colour pigments of fruits and vegetables (especially the blue and black ones like blueberries and prunes), so have your children eat a rainbow every day.

Avocados

These are a great food for children. High in vitamins, minerals, omega-9 fats and protein, they are one of the most nutritious foods that children can eat. They are ready to eat (if you buy them soft), need no preparation, no cooking, are easy for young children to pick up and scoop out, fresh and full of nutrients. Avocados are a whole natural food, with nothing added and nothing taken away. For children they are easy to eat mashed, scooped out with a spoon or spread on rice cakes. A 2016 study, published in the journal *Nutrients*, found that 'avocados are nutritionally unique among fruits in that they are lower in sugar and higher in fiber and monounsaturated fatty acids than most other fruits'.[1] They also have bland flavour, and so are ideal for giving to children as first foods. In fact, try to introduce them early as they might become an acquired taste if you leave it until later.

Smoothies

Smoothies are a nice way for children to drink their fruit. They are much better than juiced vegetables or fruit because they contain the whole of the fruit with all the soluble fibre that comes with them. It is a good idea to use a variety of berries rather than bananas, which are quite high in fruit sugar. If you do include banana, do not use a whole one. Shop-bought smoothies are not good, as they tend to limit the higher value and more expensive fruits like blueberries. Thick smoothies can be eaten with a spoon as part of a nutritious dessert.

Fresh meat

Meat has had a bad press in recent times but, along with fish and eggs, it has the highest concentration of nutrients of any food. It is rich in protein, B vitamins, vitamin A, vitamin D, vitamin K2, minerals and iron. We have eaten this food since the Stone Age so it does not deserve to be on the bad food list now. It is *not* the case that meat fat causes heart disease, and the latest thinking and research bears this out.

When we think of meat, while we picture cows grazing happily in fields and chewing the cud, this happens much less today. Nowadays most cows are kept indoors and fed a different diet from the grass-fed beef cattle of old. The nutrients in meat as well as fish and eggs depend on what the animals have been fed. One study published in the journal *Meat Science* found that organic meat had higher levels of CLA (conjugated linoleic acid) and omega-3 and a lower ratio of omega-3 to omega-6 than non-organic meat.[2] These fats are needed for the brain and so are very important.

If your child loves hamburgers, it is very easy to make natural good quality hamburgers yourself with lean organic mince, and these taste much better than those bought in shops. All you need to do is form into a patty and bake.

Although good meat is expensive, cheaper cuts such as minced meat can be cooked slowly and be just as tasty as the dearer cuts. Meat stocks are very nutritious and, with added vegetables, the resulting soups pack a huge punch in terms of nutrition.

Nuts and seeds

Fresh nuts are high in nutrients, especially magnesium and essential fatty acids. If you can, buy nuts still in their shells, as the shells will keep them fresh. Unfortunately, these tend to be sold only at Christmas time. If you do buy nuts shelled, keep them in an airtight container in the fridge, and make sure you eat them before their sell-by date.

Seeds are also highly nutritious – pumpkin, sesame, flaxseeds and sunflower seeds are all good examples. You can add seeds to your baking. You can also use groundnuts instead of flour (but do not give whole nuts to young children because of the risk of choking).

Nut butters

Nut butters are easy to use, highly nutritious and delicious.

They contain essential fatty acids, protein, and many vitamins and minerals. Try almond, hazelnut and cashew, and don't forget seed butters if you can find them.

All foods high in oil should be refrigerated and used before the sell-by date, as rancid oil is not something we should have in our bodies. Try to find nut butters that do not have added processed oils such as palm oil or too much salt. Again, we have the problem of food manufacturers making natural foods less healthy by adding in substances that are not needed.

Bean sprouts

Many children do not like Brussels sprouts, but I am referring here to a different kind of sprouts. These are bean sprouts. Certain beans and seeds – such as mung beans and alfalfa seeds – will sprout when soaked in water and then rinsed for a few days. They are not only tasty but also extremely nutritious, because as they begin their sprouting their vitamin content increases massively. Children love to sprout them themselves and then can enjoy the results when ready. Bean sprouts can be added to sandwiches, salads, soups or scrambled eggs, or can be eaten just on their own.

The problem with peanuts

Many children like peanuts and peanut butter, which is a pity because peanuts are one of the most allergenic foods around. Although they contain nutrients, the way they are grown is not always good, and they can contain the poison aflatoxin. (An interesting point about peanuts is that they are not nuts at all, but legumes.)

Coconut oil and milk

Coconut oil is the most stable oil for cooking. It can be bought in health food shops but supermarkets are now beginning to stock it. Coconut milk can be bought in cans and is useful for making curry sauces.

Millet and quinoa

These are nutritious grains. Millet is quite high in magnesium, iron and B6. Cooked millet can be combined with grated cheese and tomatoes for a tasty nutritious dish; add carrots and broccoli to quinoa for extra flavour and texture. Quinoa is one of the few grains that is high in protein. It has twice the protein content of rice or barley and is quite rich in magnesium, calcium and manganese. It can be used like rice and combined with lots of different vegetables for a healthy cooked meal.

Yogurt

Yogurt is high in calcium and other minerals and is easier to digest than milk or cheese. It also contains beneficial bacteria so is valuable for digestion. Goat's milk yogurt is digested more easily than that made from cow's milk, but has a distinctive taste.

On the other hand, there is some controversy over whether or not we should drink milk and eat dairy foods at all. Certainly there are some people who don't tolerate it very well. It has been said that humans are the only animals who will drink and eat the products of another animal. Some people feel cows' milk is a problem because cows are often milked while pregnant, so their dairy is rich in hormones like oestrogen. If you do not want to eat yogurt made from cows' or animal milks there are delicious alternatives made from coconut milk, which can be bought in health food shops.

Go organic if you can

Organic fruits and vegetables are grown without artificial fertilisers, and without pesticides to kill bugs, herbicides to kill weeds and fungicides to kill fungi. With non-organic foods, some of these chemicals stay on the crops and some have been found to cause cancer. For example, studies have found as many as eleven different pesticides on one piece of lettuce, so you can see how much our food is affected.[3] It has also been shown that organically grown produce is higher in vitamins, minerals and phytochemicals than non-organic. They have higher levels of vitamin C, iron, magnesium and phosphorus than non-organic varieties of the same foods.

They also tend to have greater amounts of plant or phyto-chemicals. For all of these reasons, I recommend that you buy organic food if you can.

It is also better to buy organic meat, chicken, milk and eggs. Ordinary chickens have a very difficult life. They are often dosed with steroids and antibiotics and kept in poor conditions. Organic farmers, on the other hand, have to stick to strict rules with regard to feeding the animals and the use of any growth hormones or antibiotics. In addition to this, organic farmers do not grow genetically modified crops. I do not recommend GM foods as we don't know enough about them.

Free range is not the same as organic. With free-range chickens, the animals can move about but this does not mean that they are necessarily better fed. All organic meat is free range but not all free range is organic, so you have to be careful about what you buy.

In a nutshell

- The best foods for your children are those that are fresh and natural.

- The list of good foods is many and varied.

- Good foods can be easy to find and to use.

- Many need no or very little preparation.

- Try to use organic food if you can.

- Soups and casseroles are particularly valuable as they include many different ingredients.

Chapter 6

A DAY'S HEALTHY EATING

We have seen just how many foods are good for us and are easy to prepare. Now, we'll look at how healthy eating might look for a whole day. This includes ideas for coping with that extremely difficult time of day: when your ravenous child returns from school!

Breakfasts

This first meal of the day comes at a very busy time, when everyone is in a panic trying to get ready and out of the door. We need something quick to make and easy to eat, and this is probably why toast and cereals are so popular. However, we discussed in Chapter 4 that every meal or snack needs to combine protein, carbohydrate and fat.

Breakfast really is a very important meal, especially for children; in fact, it is the most important meal of the day because your child is literally breaking the overnight fast. After sleeping many hours (more than an adult), their blood sugar levels will have dropped very low. We saw in Chapter 4 that low blood sugar causes all sorts of problems to do with learning, concentration and memory, as well as behaviour.

A study published in the journal *Physiology & Behaviour* looked at the effects of eating breakfast on cognitive function, mood and concentration in children aged twelve to fifteen.[1] They were divided randomly into two groups. One group was given breakfast, the other was not. They were then given various tests to complete, and it was found that those having breakfast did better and their blood sugar level was higher, as you might expect. The authors concluded that, 'the findings of the present study suggest that breakfast consumption enhances cognitive function in an adolescent population when compared to breakfast omission'.

If children don't have a good breakfast this of course increases the amount of time that they are fasting, and their blood sugar will drop even lower. Because the brain needs sugar to work properly, if they miss breakfast, they are less likely to be able to understand what they are being taught. Many studies have shown that children who have a good breakfast do better throughout the whole day. Children who were given breakfast on a near-daily basis had higher scores in IQ tests than children who 'sometimes' had breakfast. This was so even after adjusting for other factors like parents' education level or occupations.[2]

Good breakfasts

While a good breakfast will set your child on the right track for the day, a bad breakfast will raise blood sugar too high too quickly, which will be followed by a rise in insulin, and cause a drop in blood sugar a few hours later.

Sadly, a bad breakfast is what many people eat every day – cereals, milk, toast, maybe croissants and orange juice. Although this looks like a normal breakfast, it is actually extremely high in foods which turn to glucose very quickly. Refined breads act like sugar in the body and quickly cause a spike in your children's blood sugar.

A good breakfast is one that keeps your child's blood sugar stable throughout the next few hours until lunchtime. It must be easy to digest, but can be quick to prepare. In order to keep blood sugar stable for a long time, it needs to combine protein, fat and carbohydrate.

Eggs are high in protein and easy to prepare. Scrambled eggs take just a few minutes. For carbohydrate you could add a slice of rye toast and half a banana. Fat can be added in the form of butter or good nut butter. A breakfast like this should help learning and concentration dramatically.

Don't be too traditional about breakfast. There is no reason why children cannot have any good food that they like so long as it fits in with the general principle described above.

If there really is no time in the morning, why not make a few bits the night before and leave them in the fridge? Children who travel to school could eat these on the way – it's not ideal, I know, but better than them having nothing at all.

The traditional British breakfast made better

This traditional breakfast fry-up has often been seen as unhealthy, containing processed sausages and bacon and fried in bad oil. However, there are versions of this that are not as bad and can be made into a healthy meal if you are careful about what food you include and how you cook it. For example, your child could have grilled tomatoes, poached eggs, mushrooms cooked in butter and some boiled potatoes for carbohydrate. Of course, it would be difficult to go to these lengths every day, but this could be a treat at the weekend. It would certainly help keep blood sugar stable for quite a few hours.

Ideas for healthy breakfasts

- Scrambled eggs, half a banana, toast with butter.

- Good bread with cashew or almond butter, fruit.

- Smoothies made with fruit and some coconut milk to add fat and some protein.

- Porridge, egg, banana.

- Leftover meat from dinner in a sandwich with lettuce and tomato.

- Leftover chicken in a wholemeal pitta with tomatoes, nuts.

- Avocado mashed into rice cakes, with an egg.

- Good quality muesli, egg, tangerine.

- Natural whole milk yogurt with berries, toast and nut butter.

- Chopped herring on good toast, fruit.

- Millet with grated cheese and cooked tomato, nuts.

- Quinoa with grated cheese, banana.

Packed lunches

Do you find choosing healthy food for packed lunches a real ordeal?

Children used to go home for lunch, and some even had a three-course, home-cooked meal. I did this myself, but it is hard to imagine children doing this today.

Times have changed and now many children take a packed lunch. This can be good or terrible depending on what is in it. The middle of the day is the ideal time to fill small tummies with the best and most nutritious food. Children are less tired at this time, and their digestion is probably better than in the evening. If you provide the best food for them it will enhance their learning and concentration for the whole afternoon.

However, even if you prepare something great, we all know that some children are very good at using food as currency or swapping it for something 'better'. You may wonder who is actually going to be eating the lovely nutritious packed lunch that you prepared, or even worse whose unhealthy lunch *your* child will be eating! We can only try our best. If you give them good food that you know they like, it decreases the chances of this happening.

The wrong packed lunch

Some packed lunches are so bad that they do children very little good at all. They often consist of white bread sandwiches, with maybe peanut butter or cheese. Even worse, the sandwiches might be filled with chocolate spread or jam – these sandwiches contain practically nothing of any value and this will cause a dramatic sugar hit only to be followed by a slump later on.

Then there is the sweet drink, crisps or a biscuit, or both – more sugar with all its inherent problems. This will again cause the child's blood sugar to skyrocket and be followed by a dramatic slump.

A study published in the *Journal of Epidemiology and Community Health* found that just 1 per cent of the packed lunches sampled met the standards for school meals.[3] They were low in saturated fat, vitamin A, folic acid (a B vitamin), iron and zinc. Another study conducted in rural Virginia in the USA found that packed lunches were lower in salt (not a bad thing in this case), protein, fibre, vitamin A and calcium than school lunches.[4] Lunches like this will not help children to work hard, listen and learn. It will be bad for concentration in the afternoon, bad for energy after the initial sugar hit and bad for long-term brain development and health. It is a rapid road to type 2 sugar diabetes in the long term. The midday meal should be nothing like this!

But do not worry. It is possible to conjure up wonderful, healthy packed lunches with very little effort. As you'll know by now, you want a meal which includes some protein, fat and complex carbohydrate to help keep blood sugar stable, and a wide variety of nutrients. You also want something that looks and tastes nice.

Ideas for packed lunches

- Good quality thin bread with chicken and salad, fresh fruit.

- Sandwich with egg and cress, banana.

- Salad with food left over from the night before such as cold chicken, rice salad, potato salad, fish balls, cherry tomatoes.

- A nutritious hot soup in a flask. Keep the same ratio of protein, fat and carbohydrate by preparing a meat and vegetable or chicken soup with some good quality bread.

- Hardboiled egg with some cherry tomatoes, oatcakes with butter, and a small banana.

- Pitta bread, tinned sardines, tomatoes, banana.

- Piece of good quality bought quiche, fruit, cherry tomatoes.

- Wrap with fish, egg or chicken, salad, fruit.

Weekend lunches

These can be more substantial than a packed lunch and can be any good food. The dinners below can be served at lunchtime.

Feeding your ravenous after-school child

Children seem to be very hungry at this time and it is no wonder as they have been working hard all day. Brainwork requires even more glucose than physical work.

Do you wonder what you should give them at that time? Are you afraid that if you give too much they might not eat their evening meal? On the other hand, are you giving them poor quality snacks as a stopgap? After school is when children are often given crisps, biscuits or cakes. I constantly see children munching processed snacks as they walk home from school with their friends or parents. This is such a pity, because if they are hungry it is an ideal time to get something nutritious into them.

A list of healthy snacks comes below. But why not just give them part of their evening meal there and then? They can have the rest with the family later. So if their evening meal is going to be soup, meat or fish with vegetables, just give a little of these foods to take the edge off their appetite. Or what about giving them a nice vegetable soup in the cold winter months? It can be full of as many vegetables as you like, along with some meat or chicken.

And, remember, you don't have to spend hours preparing their after-school snack. Soup can keep for a few days, as can stews and casseroles or a roast chicken. Scrambled eggs take a few minutes to make, as do salads and cut up avocadoes. Poached fish also takes a few minutes.

However, this should not be their last meal of the day. They will need more food in the evening as well, otherwise they will be going too long without food and their blood sugar will drop too low during the night.

Often our eating habits are just that – habits. We get used to eating certain things at certain times, so if your children have a mini meal after school they will soon come to expect it. If children are given crisps, sweets or biscuits every day after school from the beginning this is what they will come to expect.

Dinners

This is when you can really give your child the very best combination of foods. Usually there is more time at dinner than at breakfast, and your child will be at home rather than at school. However, the idea that children have 'tea' often means that they are given a pasta dish or beans on toast, but it is much better to have the kind of food that parents would call 'dinner'. This is the ideal time for your child to have a proper two- or three-course meal. An ideal combination would consist of a bowl of homemade soup, a meat/fish protein course with vegetables and perhaps a healthy dessert.

The timing of this meal is also important. If it is given quite early then your child will need another snack half an hour to an hour before bed, depending on your child, so that their blood sugar does not drop too low during the night. If possible, parents should sit down at a table and eat with their children. It can be an enjoyable time for conversation, and children will probably enjoy eating 'grown-up' food. However, I do understand parents allowing children to eat in front of the television if this means that they will eat more food.

Dinners

• Vegetable soup, organic chicken, broccoli, carrots.

• Any soup, sardines, potatoes, cabbage, other vegetables.

• Meat, brown rice, corn, carrots.

• Salmon, broccoli, carrots, potatoes.

• Soup, fish with brown rice and vegetables.

- Eggs, vegetables, potatoes.

- Small amount of pasta with meat and lots of vegetable.

Occasional desserts

Although desserts are not needed, it is nice to have them from time to time and it is possible to make quite healthy ones. For instance:

- Fruit or fresh fruit salad – this is the best dessert, but some people cannot digest fruit well if eaten with other foods.

- Baked apples with added spices like cinnamon and cloves (which have important anti-cancer properties).

- Creamed coconut mixed with cocoa, and a few table-spoons of orange juice to sweeten it.

- A sponge topping for an apple pie made with a small amount of sugar, eggs and butter and whole-wheat flour can be an occasional treat.

- Home-made low-sugar custard.

- Natural organic yogurt.

If you do use recipes, reduce the amount of sugar they rec-ommend to half. As your family gets used to eating less sugar this will be quite acceptable.

Before bed

If your child is eating the main meal early then he or she should have some more food half an hour to an hour before bed, as going for so long without food is not good. This should follow the rule about protein combined with fat and some carbohydrate, and a list of healthy snacks comes just below. If your child's blood sugar drops too low during the night this will cause a release of adrenalin, which could wake him up.

Snacks

Children need snacks. Some might think that snacking is a bad thing, but children should have snacks in order to keep their blood sugar stable and increase their intake of nutrients. Many parents don't approve of snacks because they feel that they will take the edge off the child's appetite and they 'won't eat their dinner'. This does not matter if the snacks are good quality. They can count as part of the dinner itself.

The problem is that the food industry has made a fortune acknowledging the fact that children need, like and want snacks, and has dreamt up an endless list of tempting and tasty morsels. These are usually very low in nutrients, extremely high in salt and contain processed oils and chemicals additives – all things that children might like, but which are very bad for them.

Our shops are overladen with every type of snack under the sun, and they are designed to be as tempting as possible. Everything a child eats should build health, and children are much better off with natural foods. Shop-bought snacks are much less healthy than just about any other type of food, but everywhere you see children walking around eating packets of crisps or other savoury or sugary snacks. Children's tummies are small, so why fill them up with things that are of little nutritional value?

Make the snacks count

Snacks can be just as nutritious as any other food, and good wholefood snacks can actually contribute hugely to children's intake of vitamins, minerals and essential fats. Children need regular food to keep their blood sugar stable, which means better energy and concentration.

Pieces of food left-over from lunch can be given later on, or try some of the following:

Ideas for snacks

- Nuts with fruit (for older children only due to the risk of choking in younger ones).

- Seeds: sunflower and pumpkin seeds.

- Good bread or rice cakes spread with homemade hummus or non-hydrogenated cashew or almond butter.

- Plain whole milk yogurt with berries.

- Pieces of hardboiled egg cut up and mashed on to good bread or rice cakes.

- Crunchy sticks of celery with nut butter in the groove.

- Baby or mini potatoes with grated cheese.

- Rice cakes with chopped herring for omega-3 fats.

- Good bread with butter and mashed egg.

- Chopped herring on bread or rice cakes.

- Chunks of cheese with bits of apple.

- Good bread or rice cakes spread with mashed avocado.

- Smoothies made with fruit and coconut milk. The latter prevents the blood sugar rising too high too quickly.

- Raw vegetables such as carrot sticks and cherry tomatoes dipped in hummus.

- Leftover chicken pieces in pitta bread.

Eating out

Many people enjoy eating out and taking their children into cafés and restaurants, and why not? It is nice for parents not to have to cook all the time. However, what can our children have that is healthy?

I still wouldn't give then huge bowls of pasta, or most things that appear on our restaurants' 'children's menus'. But what about poached eggs on toast with salad, or jacket potatoes with a good quality filling (not tuna as this often comes with far too much mayonnaise), an egg salad sandwich or one with avocado, chicken and salad?

If you are out and about and on public transport with no cafés around, it is better to find a shop that sells a takeaway sandwich or wrap obtaining some protein, than give your children a bar of chocolate or another sweet item. A small packet of unsalted nuts could be added. This will keep them going for a while without raising blood sugar too high too quickly.

Best ways of cooking

Some ways of cooking are better than others. Frying is not good because it creates free radical damage and uses processed oils. There are also arguments against the use of microwaves. Instead, keep to these cooking methods:

- Baking in the oven
- Slow cooking for meat
- Simmering
- Steaming
- Casseroling
- Stewing
- Poaching

In a nutshell

- Breakfasts literally break our overnight fast and are essential for your child's blood sugar level.

- Cereal or toast with fruit juice are bad breakfasts. Instead, make sure your meal has protein, fat and carbohydrate.

- Have nutritious foods that your children like in their packed lunch, to best discourage them from swapping it for something unhealthy.

- When your child returns home ravenous after school, rather than offer junk food it is better to give them a healthy snack or some of their dinner early.

- Refined sugar and products made from it should be kept out of the diet. Eating cakes, biscuits, sweets and other sugary foods causes low blood sugar and so either cut these out or keep them down to a minimum. If your children do want something sweet, it should be with a meal rather than on its own. Snacks should not be sugary unless accompanied by some protein and fat.

- Make sure your child has something to eat half an hour to an hour before bed, so that their blood sugar does not drop too low during the night. Try to avoid frying or using the microwave.

Chapter 7

VITAMIN D

Should you give children supplements? If you go into health food shops there seem to be more supplements than shampoos at the chemist. Are there any which your children need or could benefit from? In my view, food must come first and you cannot replace real food with pills. However, certain supplements are valuable, and vitamin D is essential.

Vitamin D

Do you remember being given cod liver oil or vitamin drops as a child? This was given free to all children after the Second World War in order to prevent rickets, a disease where the bones become bent and bowed. Orange juice was also included, and I have to say that it tasted much better than the cod liver oil! Children were given these as sources of vitamin D (cod liver oil) and vitamin C (orange juice). Later children were given drops of vitamins A and D.

Vitamin D is the one supplement that is truly needed. It is very difficult to get this nutrient from food, and research has shown that most people living in cold climates are deficient in this vital substance. Strangely enough, research has also shown that many people living in hot climates are also deficient.

Actually, vitamin D is not really a vitamin at all but a steroid hormone which has many functions in the body. Vitamin D has become big news and that is because it is involved in so many bodily processes. It is needed in order to absorb the minerals calcium and phosphorus for healthy bones and teeth, it helps the immune system, and low levels are implicated in diseases like diabetes and even cancer.

Because it helps calcium to be absorbed into the bones, it prevents the awful bone deformity rickets as well as osteoporosis in adults. It is a long time since children were given cod liver oil free from the government, but rickets has come back and there is now a worldwide epidemic. A study publishes in the *Journal of Pediatric Endocrinology* found that out of their sample of 440 children and adolescents in Turkey, 40 per cent were found to have low levels of vitamin D, and this was especially bad in adolescent girls.[1] Children still need to be given supplements today.

Where does vitamin D come from?

Vitamin D is not easy to obtain. There is very little found

in food. It is made by sunlight on the skin, but the problem is that in the northern regions we get very little sun. As Scottish comedian Billy Connolly has said, in the sun he takes a week to go white, having begun blue with cold. Even in the summer, men and women both wear trousers, and children are now covered up for fear of getting skin cancer. In addition, vitamin D is made on the oil of our skin, but with frequent washing there is sometimes very little skin oil available for this to happen. Of course, it is important to be careful in the sun, especially at midday, but we do need to get some natural sunlight every day. I was fascinated to read that the modern trend of shopping in malls or covered centres, rather than outside in the fresh air, means that we are getting even less vitamin D than we used to. This had never occurred to me.

Parents of very young children are now told how important it is to give vitamin D drops to their babies and toddlers. If they are bottle fed wait until that has stopped, as formula milk will contain it already. The Department of Health recommends that children be given supplements from age six months to four years.[2]

A study in the *Journal of Paediatric Gastroenterology Nutrition* found that it is common for otherwise healthy children to be deficient in vitamin D.[3] This deficiency was more common in breast-fed infants (probably because bottled milk is fortified), obese children, children living in northern countries and those who lack enough sun exposure. The recommendation is that children in the above groups may need supplementation after one year.

Those with darker skins need more vitamin D and should be exposed to the sun some of the time. Of course, it is important not to burn, but some sun exposure is important.

A general vitamin/mineral complex with vitamin D

The vitamin D that I am referring to is vitamin D3 or 25-hydroxy vitamin D (25-OH vitamin D). As you are giving vitamin D anyway, you could buy a tablet that contains other vitamins, as a kind of insurance policy.

Chapter 8

WHAT NOT TO FEED YOUR CHILDREN

We are sometimes told that there are no bad foods, just bad diets. That if we eat a generally good diet, we can eat a little of any food we like. Don't be fooled by this. There certainly are bad foods, and they are mainly those that have been heavily promoted by the food industry. Bad foods can either take up space in our children's stomachs giving nothing in return, or they can be downright harmful.

Bad foods are even worse for children than adults, because children need more nutrients relative to their size. They are growing fast, but their tummies are relatively small. This means that there is no room for foods that don't have much value, and dangerous chemicals may have a more powerful effect. On top of this, some children do not want very much to eat or can be fussy eaters, so every mouthful of food has to earn its place in their diet. This chapter discusses the foods which are not good for children and are best avoided altogether.

Processed meats

'Processed meats' refers to meat that has been transformed by salting, curing, smoking or fermenting. It includes luncheon meat, bologna, salami, sausages, spam, ham, hot dogs, pastrami, beef jerky, corned beef, tinned meat and pre-packed slices of processed chicken and turkey. These products are usually made from poorer quality meat, and have added salt, nitrites and colours, along with other additives. Avoid them at all costs. They are not good for adults, and even worse for children. In 2007, the World Cancer Research Fund and the *American Institute for Cancer Research* reviewed more than seven thousand clinical studies and concluded that no amount of processed meat is safe and that no one should eat it.[1]

Highly salted foods

Even though we do need some salt, today's processed foods are loaded with this condiment. The chemical name for salt is sodium chloride, and sodium needs to be in balance with the mineral potassium. Potassium is found in all fresh fruits and vegetables, whereas sodium is found naturally in just a few foods (and at lower levels). If we think about what we would have eaten before factories and shops existed, we can see that salt would have been a very scarce commodity. In the natural state, we would have had much more potassium than sodium as we would have eaten far more fresh fruits and vegetables than we do now. In addition to this, we would not have had all the processed salty foods that we have today. The only salt consumed would have been that found naturally in food such as fish, celery and beets, but the proportions would have been very different. Although human milk contains sodium, it contains three times as much potassium, and this gives an indication of how much we really need.

Nowadays we ingest huge amounts of salt or sodium in all sorts of foods. One study published in the journal *Hypertension* found that children in south London aged ten to twelve had an intake of salt well above the recommended level.[2] The salt was coming from foods like cereal and cereal-based products (34 per cent), meat products (19 per cent) and milk and milk products (11 per cent). It is interesting that there is no mention of crisps and other salty snacks in this particular study, although these contribute hugely to most children's daily intake.

Levels of salt that are too high can cause high blood pressure (hypertension), and in adults this has been known about for a long time. Until recently, high blood pressure was not usually seen to be a problem in children, but a study in Croatia found older children and adolescents were actually now suffering from this condition.[3] This should not be happening. Another British study in the *Journal of Human Hypertension* concluded that: 'Currently, salt intake in young people is unnecessarily high due, in most countries, to hidden salt added to food by the food industry. The high salt intake may predispose them to develop high blood pressure later in life.'[4]

Salt is in just about everything that you don't make yourself. Even foods that don't actually taste salty, like bread and cereals, can contain too much of it. On top of that, we often add more salt to food via the saltshaker, so this adds up to a huge amount overall. The answer is to cut down on processed foods as much as possible and add more foods rich in potassium, like fresh fruit and vegetables (without added salt).

Processed sugar

It has been known for decades that processed sugar is bad for children and everyone else, but it is only very recently that the government and health officials have paid it very much attention. Sugar used to be called 'the white death' and according to Dr Natasha Campbell-McBride, a doctor and nutritionist and expert on autism, it deserves this title 100 per cent.[5] By sugar, I mean the white crystalline substance that we put in tea and coffee and which is used to sweeten biscuits, cakes, yogurts and a whole host of other foods. There are no nutrients in this type of sugar; it just gives us empty calories and is a complete junk food.

What is wrong with sugar?

The media home into the problem of obesity and its link to sugar, and this is certainly important, but it is not the only way that sugar affects us. Refined sugar is associated with many other health problems such as type 2 diabetes, which itself has important consequences for health. Type 2 diabetes used to be called 'adult onset diabetes' because it was not common to get the disease until adulthood. However, now children are getting it at ever-younger ages.

Too much refined sugar is also implicated in heart disease and even cancer. It causes a dramatic rise in glucose, which results in a slump a few hours later, and causes tooth decay. It gives us calories but no nutrition, and it can be addictive. A study published in the journal *Neuroscience & Biobehavioral Reviews* found that rats given sugar water have become addicted to it.[6]

We all know that sweet foods such as chocolate, desserts, cakes and biscuits are loaded with sugar. Fizzy drinks can include eleven teaspoons of sugar per 500ml bottle. However, we may not realise that sugar is added to many other foods that do not taste particularly sweet. For example, it is added to just about every processed food that is sold in the supermarket, including ready meals, salad dressings, pasta sauces, soups, chopped herring, baked beans, soups, meat dishes – and tomato ketchup can contain more sugar than ice cream! In the bakery, we know it is in cakes, but it is also added to breads and pizzas.

Children like sweetness even more than adults. Breast milk is sweet and fruit is sweet when ripe. We need to eat fruit, because along with the sweetness come vitamins, minerals and many plant chemicals that are anti-cancer and anti-inflammatory. However, we have managed to process out the sweetness from sugar beet and sugar cane or fruit, leaving behind the nutrients that come naturally with it. So instead of having fruit itself, we have the most sickly gooey chemical-laden rubbish manufacturers can dream up. It also comes under a number of different aliases, such as:

- Sucrose

- Dextrose

- Fructose

- Glucose

- Maltose

- Laevulose

- Corn sweetener

- Invert sugar

- Molasses

- Syrup

- High-fructose corn syrup

- Maple syrup

We don't need refined sugar

Some parents think that children need some sugar for energy, but this is not the case with white processed sugar or sucrose. There are natural sugars in milk, fruits and vegetables, and these come combined with the vitamins and minerals needed to metabolise them as well as other important nutrients. White processed sugar or sucrose has none of these. Because it does not contain any nutrients of its own, it depends on other vitamins to process it, so it actually takes away nutrients from our other foods.

You might think that some types of refined sugar are better than others, but don't be fooled. Refined sugars such as fruit sugar, brown sugar and muscovado sugar are all still sugar. Although molasses contains some natural minerals like iron, it is still sugar and we do not need it. Honey has some nutrients, but it is mainly just sugar.

Giving up refined sugar

This is not difficult for children if they are young. And if they are very young, they may never have been introduced to it at all. There is enough natural sweetness in fruit and some vegetables to keep our blood sugar stable. This, together with the starches in potatoes and rice, gives us all the sugar we need.

Of course, your children may have sweets available to them when they are away from you, but you can keep your home sugar free. Chapter 12 discusses the tricky issue of parties.

If you have older children and are introducing this change, try and explain why better nutrition is good for them. Chapter 14 offers help with this.

As mentioned above, sugar can become addictive, and the more we have the more we want. On the other hand, if we stop eating it for a while our sweet tooth can diminish. If you give up sugar and then eat something very sweet, it starts to taste sickly and unappealing. Having said this, it is very important to keep blood sugar even by eating naturally sweet things with protein, as discussed in Chapter 4.

Which sugars do we need?

Nature has provided us with lots of naturally sweet foods, and we do not need to process sugar out artificially and add it to foods like meat dishes that should not include it.

Breast milk is naturally sweet and contains the milk sugar lactose. And children can have the natural sugars in fruit, dried fruit and vegetables like potatoes. The starch in foods like rice and wholemeal bread is also converted to glucose, so your child will not miss out.

If your children want something sweet, do give them fruit or dried fruit. After all, we probably have a sweet tooth in order to encourage us to eat fruit, which gives us vitamins, minerals and many plant chemicals along with the sweet taste. Fruit also becomes sweet when it is ripe, as a sign for us that it is ready to eat. For occasional desserts, see Chapter 6.

Sugar substitutes

There are many artificial sugar substitutes in our foods but these are just chemicals that do nothing for your children's health. In addition to this, it is better if children (and adults) start to prefer savoury foods rather than those that have a sweet, sugary taste.

Processed oils and fats

Just about everything in the supermarket contains sunflower oil, corn oil or rapeseed oil, or the hard fats made from them (such as all margarines). These oils are very new to our diet, and are highly processed, going through many processes including boiling, bleaching, deodorising and defoaming. Eating these fats is one of the worst changes that we have made to our diet since time began.

It is astonishing just how many foods come into this category. If you go round the supermarket and read labels, you will see that just about everything that is not totally fresh contains them. As a result our bodies have become saturated with them and they take the place of the healthy fats that we need to get from oily fish and fresh nuts and seeds. There are two problems here:

1. We eat far too much omega-6 in relation to omega-3.
2. The omega-6 that we are getting is so changed by processing that it causes all sorts of health problems. In children, it can affect the brain.

Processed oils are in crisps (including vegetable crisps), most savoury snacks, chips, samosas, cakes, biscuits, breads, crackers, many breakfast cereals, ice cream, artificial cheese, whipped toppings, ready meals, pizzas, taramasalata, hummus, fried fish, all other fried foods, goujons, onion rings, desserts, chocolate, mayonnaise, salad cream, bought soups, margarines, other spreads, cook-in-sauces, non-dairy creamers, all oils except extra virgin olive oil and coconut oil, pasta sauces, dips, ready prepared rice, chopped herring, chopped liver and fish tinned in oil. Strangely enough, even raisins contain oil – to keep them from sticking together.

You can see just how difficult it is to avoid these bad oils unless you make most of your food yourself.

Margarine

As if boiling, bleaching, deodorising and defoaming isn't enough – for hard fats like margarine there is more. After defoaming the oil is still liquid, but manufacturers want a product that looks and spreads like butter, so they blast it with hydrogen atoms. Now we have a hydrogenated fat or a trans fat, and these are bad for us.

There is a very interesting story related to this. As butter has always been expensive to produce, requiring cows and good grazing land, Napoleon III wanted to find a cheap substitute, so he offered a prize to anyone who could make one. Margarine was the result. It might have been cheap, but it was and is nothing like butter in terms of goodness or nutrition. It has been controversial from the start, and was banned for many years under Canadian law.

It used to be thought that vegetable oils and margarine were good for us because they were low in saturated fat, but we now know that the fat in processed oils is not good. The sad thing is that some people eat more of them, as they still believe they are good for us.

In a nutshell

- Children need a high level of nutrients but have small stomachs so there is no room for unhelpful foods.

- They should not be given processed meats like spam, hot dogs, sausages or salami. The meat children eat should come from grass-fed organically raised animals.

- Children need some salt but should not be given highly salted foods; many foods sold in supermarkets come into this category. Beware of hidden salt in foods that do not taste salty.

- They should not eat refined sugar or foods containing this, such as sweets, biscuits and cakes. There is quite a lot of sugar in savoury foods like bread and tomato ketchup.

- Processed oils and fats such as sunflower, corn, rapeseed and canola – and all foods made from them – should not be eaten as they compete with good fats in the body.

- Margarine is also a very bad food and is contained in many processed foods and recipes for cakes and desserts. Butter is better.

Chapter 9

FOODS SOLD AS 'HEALTHY' THAT ARE NOT

We all want to help our children be as healthy as possible. Manufacturers know this, and try to dream up new foods that appear to fit in with this desire and market them to health-conscious parents. However, the truth is that many foods that are marketed as healthy are quite the opposite. Often heavily processed, high in sugar and salt, they are given the label 'healthy' because they may contain a few added vitamins or minerals or may have reduced fat. This makes us think that they are good for our children, but often they are not. Don't be fooled by them, and don't waste your money on these marketing ploys.

But in reality we are all vulnerable to marketing, and this chapter discusses in more detail the foods most often advertised as 'healthy'.

Some foods labelled as 'low fat'

Have you been led to believe that fat is bad, causes heart disease and makes us put on weight? This myth has been promoted for decades. As Chapter 3 explained, the latest research suggests that fat is not bad if eaten in natural foods. However, many parents still believe that it is, and manufacturers still make many products labelled 'low fat', hoping that this will attract more customers. All sorts of foods come into this category: cakes, biscuits, yogurts, spreads, milk and so on.

One problem is that low fat foods are often so processed and so lacking in taste that extra sugar is added to make them more appealing. You may have noticed that many of these low fat foods are much sweeter than the 'normal' variety. They should be avoided.

But that is not the main problem with 'low fat' foods. The main problem is that good foods contain nutrients we need. If a food is right for us, it is right whether it is low fat or not. For example, an avocado contains a fair amount of fat, but we need fat in our diet and the natural fat in avocados is good for us. This is also true of whole fat milk. Milk is a whole food: nothing added and nothing taken away. Whole fat milk is better for children than low fat milk, because fat in milk helps the absorption of calcium, so it is not a good idea to give children skimmed milk or low fat yogurt. The whole of the food is high in vitamins, minerals and the natural monounsaturated fat that we need.

Biscuits are often sold as 'low fat' but are not good for children (or adults) whether they are low in fat or not. Often they are high in sugar to make up for the lack of taste and, as mentioned, they can be sweeter than ordinary biscuits. Biscuits anyway are processed foods made from white flour that contain very little nutrition. It is best to avoid them.

Children should not eat low fat spreads. In fact they should not eat spreads at all. Just keep to butter.

Low sugar or diet fizzy drinks

I have just said that sugar is bad for us, so I hope you don't think that I am recommending *high* sugar drinks here. I am not! It is just that some people think that low sugar or diet fizzy drinks are fine because they don't contain sugar or contain less of it. This is not true. I would say that all fizzy drinks or squashes are bad for children as they usually contain artificial sweeteners, colourings, flavourings and other chemicals that may affect your children's health. These chemicals include phosphoric acid, which can rot the enamel on the teeth and may prevent good bone density. It used to be a fun thing for dental students to leave some teeth in a cola drink and find that they had completely *dissolved* after a time – so while it is quite good for cleaning your bath or showerhead, it is not so good for hydrating your children.

Whether they have added sugar or not, fizzy drinks should be avoided. It is much better for children to get into the habit of thinking of water as their main drink, or very diluted fresh fruit juice. For a hot drink, children could have broths, soups and herb teas as long as they don't contain artificial flavourings.

Most breakfast cereals

Have you noticed just how many different types of cereal are being sold in supermarkets? There is a vast number and they take up a huge amount of space in most food shops. They are seen by many parents as a quick and easy choice for breakfast. Often, they are seen as healthy, and some are even called 'healthy whole grains' to make them sound better than the more processed cereals such as corn flakes. But they are not healthy at all, although it is easy to understand why so many people think they are.

Most of them are just like sweets: full sugar and trans fats. A study published in the *Journal of the American Dietetic Association* looked at 161 cereals sold in the US, 46 per cent of which were seen as being marketed to children.[1] They found that cereals for children were denser in energy (calories), sugar and sodium (salt) and less dense in fibre and protein, and 66 per cent were higher in sugar than the amount recommended for health. Some are no better than sweets.

Some of these cereals are fortified with vitamins and this might lead people to think that they are good for children. However, you might ask why they need extra vitamins at all if they are good foods to start with? A natural food like a banana or carrot does not need added vitamins, because it already has the natural nutrients that nature gave it. This is important because our bodies can absorb the vitamins in natural foods more easily than synthetic vitamins added to cereal or other foods.

Most cereals, except porridge and some mueslis, are highly processed, full of sugar and other additives, and should not be seen as good food for children. They are really sweets in disguise and will cause your child's blood sugar to begin rising too high at the very beginning of the day. This will be followed by a slump a few hours later with all the unpleasant symptoms that go with it. Much better foods can be given to children at the beginning of the day. Look again at the breakfast ideas section in Chapter 6.

High-fibre cereals

Some health-conscious parents are feeding their children too much fibre. We are often told that fibre is good for us, that it prevents constipation and takes excess cholesterol and oestrogen out of our bodies. To some extent this is true, but children can have too much, especially if it comes from grains or high-bran cereals. Some parents may believe that the more fibre the better, but this is not the case.

There are different types of fibre: soluble, which means that it dissolves in water; or insoluble, which does not. Foods that contain soluble fibre are fresh fruits and vegetables, and insoluble fibre is contained in bran and wheat-based foods. Insoluble fibre is less good for children as it binds to minerals and can take these out of the body. As the modern diet tends to be low in minerals anyway, this just exacerbates the problem. High-bran cereals should not be given to children for this reason. Cereals like porridge and millet are better, as these contain fibre that is more soluble.

Cereal or oat bars

In an attempt to get us to buy their goods, manufacturers have tried to produce bars that appear to be healthy and full of goodness. Bars made from cereals come into this category. We have seen that cereals themselves are not as healthy as manufacturers would have us believe, and cereal bars are even worse. In addition to this, if you look carefully at the ingredients you will see that they often contain high levels of sugar in different forms, including syrups. High fructose corn syrup is one of the worst types of sugar that we can eat. It is not needed in a healthy diet but is included in so many foods nowadays that it is often difficult to avoid it – but it is important for your child's health that you do.

One bar I have noticed that is marketed as healthy contains nothing of any value except oats, and I was astounded to see that it also includes *six different kinds of sugar*, including dextrose and glucose syrup. How can it be legal to imply that this is a healthy snack? Another has four. These products have been marketed as a quick and easy way to have some sort of breakfast for people who are on the run. However, they are no better than a chocolate bar, and much more expensive!

It is much better for children to get used to eating real food as snacks. Half an avocado is a much better snack than a factory-made food. See Chapter 6 for a list of healthy snack foods.

Fruit drinks and high fruit squashes

Some manufacturers produce substances that are labelled 'fruit drinks' rather than 'fruit juice'. These are called 'drinks' because they are not completely natural. Those labelled 'high in fruit' may be higher in fruit than other processed drinks, but they are still very bad. Many fruit drinks contain a fair amount of sugar as well as artificial colourings and flavourings, and they should be avoided. A study published in the *British Medical Journal* found that, 'habitual consumption of sugar sweetened beverages was associated with a greater incidence of type 2 diabetes'.[2] They also said that 'artificially sweetened beverage or fruit juice were unlikely to be healthy alternatives'.

All of these drinks and squashes are high in sugar and are actually processed foods marketed as natural. It is better for children to drink water or a 100 per cent natural fruit juice diluted half-and-half with water. However, one fresh fruit juice a day is enough. Although 100 per cent fresh fruit juice seems like a healthy food, it is actually very high in natural sugars. If you think about how fresh orange juice is made, you will see that the juice from quite a few oranges is needed to get one cup. This comes with all the sugar that is in the fruit. It would be better to eat a whole orange and drink water.

Vegetable crisps

Nowadays we can buy crisps made from vegetables other than potatoes. Because they are made from vegetables and we know that vegetables are good for us, some might think that these crisps are too. However, there is not enough vegetable content to do any good, and even if there was they are fried in processed oil and full of salt. They are not really any better than ordinary crisps. However, if you want to make crispy vegetables yourself, you can slice them thinly, toss in a little olive oil and bake them in the oven.

Banana chips

These sound like something healthy and you may be drawn to them because they are made from fruit, but this is just another marketing ploy. These are either baked or fried and often highly sweetened. The amount of banana in them is tiny and will not do your child very much good. Fresh bananas have enough sweetness in themselves and so make an ideal snack without being fried. However, I would not give a whole one to a young child because it will raise blood sugar too quickly. A rice cake with nut butter and half a banana makes a nutritious snack.

Some organic foods

We are always being told that organic food is better for us and research has shown that this is the case. As mentioned elsewhere, I recommend that you buy organic food if you can.

However just because a food is organic does not mean that it is good for us or our children. There are plenty of foods on the market that are just bad, and they are not made better because they are organic. You can buy organic junk foods, such as pizzas, sweets, cakes, biscuits and even ice cream. Many of these are just as high in sugar, salt and processed oils as the non-organic varietals, so don't be fooled by them.

If sugar is bad, then organic sugar is just as bad; if crisps are bad, then organic crisps are bad too. Essentially, processed foods are bad for us whether or not the raw ingredients are organic. Being organic means that there will be fewer pesticides attached to them but they still suffer from all the problems of junk foods, if that is what they are.

Peanuts

These are not nuts at all but legumes and they can cause problems for some people. Children seem to like peanut butter and many parents see it as an easy and convenient way to get some protein into them. However, peanuts can be very allergenic and can contain a dangerous mould called aflatoxin.

Peanut butter is even worse because it has added salt and usually hydrogenated fats and palm oil. It is best to keep away from it.

Having said this nuts and nut butters are very nutritious. For fresh nuts, you can choose from almonds, cashews, walnuts, Brazil and pecan nuts. Of course, they are better fresh and not roasted or salted. Nut butters such as cashew and almond are much better than peanut butter, but keep them very fresh, as rancid oil is not something we want in our bodies.

Too much pasta

One of the reasons that I decided to write this book was that I was sitting in a cafe one day and I chanced to look to my right. Sitting there was a young child being fed a large bowl of pasta. Then I looked to my left, where there was another child also being fed a large bowl of pasta. Both of these dishes had hardly any sauce and no vegetables. This is how many children are being fed today. What they were really eating were just large bowls of starch. I know pasta is easy to cook, cheap and that children like it, but it is just a filler and does not provide much that is good. It takes the place of more nutritious foods, is hard to digest and can cause other problems.

Parents might think it is a valuable food because it is low in fat, and if it is made from wholemeal flour it is seen as one of the 'healthy whole grains'. However, most pasta is also low in just about every nutrient that your child needs. Let's think for a moment what pasta actually is. It is made from wheat, and wheat in its natural form has three parts: the germ where all the nutrients are stored; the bran, which is fibrous; and the starch, which contains very few nutrients. In order to make white pasta, the germ and the bran are discarded and only the starch is used. So it is a highly processed food that fills children up with starch, which converts to sugar quite quickly. It will raise blood sugar too high too quickly and cause a drop a few hours later. It also takes the place of the more important nutritious foods like vegetables, meat, eggs and fish. There are many forms of pasta: noodles, fettuccini, spaghetti and so on.

Wheat is not the same food that we ate even twenty years ago. Researchers have messed about with the chromosomes in the plant and changed it, making it like nothing found in nature.[3] It is not a good food for children or for their parents. Some people seem to be able to tolerate it well enough, but for others the gluten in it can cause digestive problems such as wind, bloating, stomach cramps and other symptoms.

Too much wheat in general

The problem is that wheat is everywhere in our food supplies. It is included in bread, cakes, biscuits, scones, muffins, pains au chocolat, croissants, couscous, wheat germ, semolina, durum wheat, cereals, breadcrumbs, chapattis, couscous, popadoms, nans, pancakes, waffles, pizzas, rusks, matzos and many sauces. There are so many different products made from wheat it is staggering.

This means that many adults and children are eating some form of wheat all day long. They might have cereal or toast for breakfast, a biscuit mid-morning, sandwiches for lunch (very few working people or schoolchildren don't have a sandwich for lunch), a cake with afternoon tea and some sort of pasta for the evening meal.

So what is wrong with wheat?

1. Wheat itself is a highly processed food. The gluten in it makes it very difficult to digest and can cause a whole host of problems, from coeliac disease to many autoimmune conditions like thyroid problems.

2. It takes the place of much more nutritious foods like vegetables. We need to eat many more of these in our diet. Five a day is not enough.

3. Foods made from white flour contain few nutrients. Wholewheat flour can be even worse, as it contains even higher levels of gluten than white flour.

There are those who advise eating no wheat at all and this is something that adults might try to do. However, it might be too difficult to put children onto this type of diet unless there is a good reason for it.

Instead, I advise not making wheat the main part of your child's diet, so that they are not eating it regularly through-out the day. Try to include a much wider variety of different foods, and don't give wheat in some form for every meal and snack. Great ideas for varied snacks can be found in Chapter 6.

Gluten-free foods

Many people are intolerant to the gluten in wheat, and gluten-free foods have been manufactured for people who suffer from this. Although gluten is not the only problem with wheat, many people find it difficult to tolerate this sub-stance, so the food industry produces breads, pasta, biscuits, etc. using other types of flour such as potato starch, rice starch and tapioca flour. The impression created is that they are good for us because they contain no gluten, but they are not as good as they seem. Most foods labelled 'gluten free' are highly processed, contain very few vitamins and minerals, and are full of artificial additives. If your child is intolerant to wheat, it is better to use plain ordinary foods like organic potatoes, other root vegetables and fruits as their source of carbohydrates. If you want something wheat free that you can use for nut butters or other healthy spreads and toppings try plain rice cakes, which are far less processed (if not particularly nutritious).

Quorn

Vegetarians often find it difficult to find good sources of protein to give their children so some serve Quorns thinking that it is a nutritious food. Unfortunately, this is not the case. It is a highly processed food and, although it is made from mushrooms, we do not know enough about the processing. We should cat foods in their natural state as much as possible. This is because whole natural foods contain both the important nutrients we know that we need, but will also have nutrients we have not identified, which we therefore cannot reproduce these in processed foods.

Most processed desserts

People talk about 'desserts to die for'. They might be right about that, because most of them are high in sugar and usually full of processed fat and flour as well. Most people are aware that sweet desserts are not particularly healthy, but many still feel that it is normal and natural to have some sort of pudding or dessert after meals. It might be the norm, but it isn't natural, especially when it comes to processed deserts.

For example, ice cream and cakes are high in sugar and (even worse) processed vegetable fat. Jelly is just flavoured sugar with colouring. Also, if you go on holidays where you see huge buffets, the desserts may look wonderful but often you find that many of them taste awful. This is because the cream in them is not real but instead processed fats made from one of the biggest health hazards this century – vegetable oil.

But even traditional home-made cakes and deserts contain processed sugar and flour. The best desserts are fresh fruit or fruit salads, provided that there are no digestive problems. See Chapter 6 for other healthy dessert ideas.

Artificial additives

Thousands of chemicals have been added to so many food products on offer today. They are intended to make poor food look better, taste better or keep longer, but this does not make them good for us. These additives include dyes, food colourings, artificial flavourings and sweeteners, preservatives, different kinds of sugars and many other things that we do not need. Researcher Dr Alex Richardson has said that the UK still allows some artificial additives that are banned in other EU countries.[4] She makes the point that we really do not know the effects of a variety of different additives combined together.

A study at the University of Liverpool looked at four additives: monosodium glutamate, the colours quinoline yellow and brilliant blue, and the sweetener aspartame.[5] They found that each of these prevented immature nerve cells from branching out as they otherwise would. But the combined effects of these additives in stunting nerve-cell growth were indeed synergistic, causing up to four times the effects that would be expected.

I advise that you do not need to give your children foods with added chemicals. In this book, I am trying to show parents how to feed children in the best, easiest and natural way possible. This is the way that people were fed in the past so it is not a new idea. The problem is that it is not always easy to avoid these additives, especially when eating out. However, I urge you to try.

Food colourings

In a study conducted on the Isle of Wight, researchers from the University of Southampton looked at the effect of certain artificial colourings on children's behaviour.[6] The parents were asked to remove them from their children's diets for one week, and this resulted in a dramatic improvement in behaviour. However, the researchers were careful about drawing conclusions from this alone, because the parents could have been anticipating and possibly influencing the result. To counteract this the children were then given a drink which contained additives every day for a week, and then an additive-free drink for another week. The important thing was that no one knew which was which (called a 'double blind' trial, as neither the children, the parents nor the researchers knew which drinks contained the additives). The results were similar to those in the previous study. The children having the drinks with added chemicals were more hyperactive than when on the benign drink, according to parental assessment. After the Isle of Wight study, food colouring was banned or restricted in Norway, Denmark and the US, but not in the UK. However, you can of course just ban them yourself.

As you know, I think that it is best to give all children natural, home-cooked food. We do not really know enough about additives but I advise you to keep them out of your child's diet as much as possible. Why do we need them anyway? The natural colours and flavours of fresh whole foods are much better and contain the nutrients and phytochemicals that our children need. It is only if we veer away from fresh natural food that artificial colours and flavours come into the picture at all.

Natural spices like cinnamon, cloves, ginger and turmeric have many health-giving properties and are anti-cancer and anti-inflammatory. Cinnamon is a wonderful spice which in biblical times was held to be more precious than gold. It can even be added to savoury dishes like meat.

If you stick to the diet recommended in this book, you should be relatively safe from artificial additives. If you do buy any other foods, be careful to check the labels. Is it a strawberry yogurt because real strawberries have been added, or is it laced with artificial strawberry flavouring? It is not easy to be perfect in this and you might slip up, but the aim is to do the best you can.

Is there anything left?

You might now feel that there is very little left to eat! I apologise for this, but I can assure you that there is. All of the foods above are relatively new to our diet. We have become used to them over the years, but they are not needed and we can do much better without them. It just needs a different way of thinking about food. The real food that I recommend is much tastier and more enjoyable than these highly processed products and I am sure that when you cut these out you will never want to go back to them. See Chapters 5 and 6 for many quick, easy and tasty ideas. The foods we should eat are fresh fruits and vegetables, fresh meats, eggs, fish, nuts and seeds, some good grains like millet and quinoa, and maybe yogurt (depending on whether or not your child can tolerate dairy products).

In a nutshell

- Don't be fooled by foods that are sold as healthy when they are not. These include low fat products (which can be processed and higher in sugar), low sugar products high in artificial additives and even processed organic foods.

- It is better to keep away from most breakfast cereals as they are high in sugar, salt and are usually heavily processed. Natural porridge oats are better.

- Try not to give your child too many wheat-based foods. There are so many of these on the market that children are living on them. Reduce these and use natural vegetables and a wider variety of foods instead.

- Gluten-free foods are not nutritious as they are heavily processed. They are fine for an occasional meal.

- The only fruit drink given should be diluted fresh fruit juice. Other fruit drinks containing sugar and artificial sweeteners or other additives should not be given to children.

- Fabricated foods such as Quorn are not good and it is better to eat fresh natural foods.

- Try to avoid all foods with artificial additives such as colourings and flavourings. These can affect children, and we do not yet know what combinations of different additives can do.

Chapter 10

MARKETING FOOD FOR CHILDREN

If I were to ask you what children's food is, or what is considered as children's food, you would have no hesitation in answering. This is because certain foods are deemed suitable or right for children. However, the concept of special food for children is part of a whole industry that has grown up in which children are targeted as consumers. Foods are sold like this as a marketing ploy; for material gain, not to make children healthier. Children do not need their own food – and so-called 'children's food' is much unhealthier than food marketed to adults.

We have all asked for the children's menu and seen listed fish fingers, chips, hamburgers, jelly, ice cream and so on. These foods are cheap for the restaurant, but as you will know by now they are not good for the children. When my children were small, I asked waiters instead for just smaller portions of the adult food. They looked at me in amazement. But it is not right that children, whose bodies and brains are still growing and developing, are expected to eat foods that are less nutritious than those offered to adults.

Bribery and corruption

Restaurants also entice children by giving them fancy plates, toys and crayons, but the food on offer is not going to do them any good at all. It is usually high in salt, high in processed fats, full of additives and low in nutrients. For example, a typical meal might be fish fingers, beans and chips. There is very little nutrition in this. The chips are fried in bad oil, there is very little fish in the fingers, and they usually have added salt, colourings and other chemicals; and tinned beans are high in sugar and salt too. Chicken nuggets are fried in processed oil and are also high in salt and other additives. However, these foods are seen as being right for children.

I remember a mother telling me that she had been on a cruise with her family and was upset because there was nothing her children could eat. This seemed very odd to me, because on a cruise ship the buffets are massive. They offer every possible healthy food you can think of, all sorts of meat, fish and vegetarian dishes, as well as every vegetable, and salads. However, she did not expect her children to eat that healthy food, but wanted fish fingers and other junk food instead.

Why do we think that this type of food should be given to children? Is it because it is easier? Cheaper? It should not be like this. Children's food should be just as natural and nutritious as adult food. If we think about it, it needs to be even more so given their greater needs and smaller stomachs.

In the West we fall for these marketing ploys, but elsewhere in the world children eat their indigenous food, whatever that might be. It could be curry in India or spicy food in China. Why in the West is it so different? The answer, of course, is marketing and economics. Children are seen as big consumers in the retail market and everything that is marketed to adults is marketed in a different form to children. This includes holidays, games, furniture, clothes, leisure activities and so on, and food is no exception.

The food industry has cottoned on to the fact that huge profits can be made from selling to children, who are targeted as consumers in their own right. When it comes to food, they are not promoting fresh vegetables but low quality junk foods, high in sugar, bad fats, chemical additives and few nutrients. Children do not need these foods.

Children are targeted by manufacturers

The Institute of Medicine in the United States has warned of the dangers of food marketing to children. One group of researchers looked at techniques of marketing (high sugar) cereals to children and found that they use advertising games ('advergames'), videos and site registration, among other techniques.[1] They also used viral marketing that encouraged friends to join the site. These all can create potentially huge growth in consumption.

A 2015 study found that, 'food advertising is prevalent, it promotes largely energy dense, nutrient poor foods, and even short term exposure results in children increasing their food consumption'.[2] Another study published in the journal *Public Health Nutrition* from Australia found that 157 discrete products were marketed to children via packaging, and most were foods high in fat and sugar.[3] They also found that more than sixteen different marketing techniques were used to encourage people to buy them. Another study there found that they used the technique of branded education, competitions, promotional characters, branded games and designated children's websites.[4] Again, they were skewed towards unhealthy foods in general.

Children like sweetness even more than adults. Breast milk is sweet and fruit is sweet when ripe; and we need the sweetness in fruit because along with that come vitamins, minerals and many plant chemicals that are anti-cancer and anti-inflammatory. However, as I have said, we have managed to process out the sweetness from sugar beet and sugar cane or fruit leaving behind the natural nutrients. So instead of having fruit itself they have the most sickly gooey chemical-laden rubbish manufacturers can dream up. Sugar is also added to many foods in the supermarket, even savoury ones like meat dishes or soup.

But children should not need to have special food. They should have smaller portions of the best fresh natural food that healthy adults are expected to eat.

Marketing and obesity

Marketing to children is one factor that contributes to the rise in obesity. Since children are getting fatter all the time it is important to look into the reasons for this. A 2015 study in the British medical journal *The Lancet* states that, 'The prevalence of childhood overweight and obesity has risen substantially worldwide in less than one generation.'[5] In the USA a third of children are overweight or obese and in the UK, although the numbers are not as high as this, weight is becoming a problem for more and more children. It is a major health concern for children in the developed world and children seem to be getter fatter all the time. Overweight children tend to become overweight adults, and this leads to type 2 diabetes, heart disease, cancer and a host of other conditions.

Why are children getting fatter?

This question might seem easy to answer and many theorists tell us that it is all about not getting enough exercise, sitting for too long watching the television or playing computer games. Of course, lifestyle does play a big part. It is true that many children are so occupied with television, computers and the internet that they don't play outside, running about or playing sports. It is also true that exercise is very important. But children just two decades ago had TV and read books at home, but were still much slimmer. Did they really run about so much more? Children also get exercise at school, so the rise in obesity is not just about being sedentary.

It seems that poor eating habits and the type of food eaten is by far the most important factor. This has changed dramatically in the last seventy years and now we are eating foods that our grandparents would not recognise. Adults too are getting fatter and the incidence of type 2 diabetes is skyrocketing. This is due to four main things: the huge amount of sugar they eat; the processing of fats and oils; the rise in ready meals, which nearly always contain added sugar; and the fact that we eat so many processed wheat-based foods. It is also related to the fact that foods are not high in the nutrients that help burn calories; and we are eating far too few real foods like vegetables.

Many of my clients have told me that they never learned to cook either at home or at school, and some are actually scared to try it in case they do it badly.

Overfed and undernourished

As discussed in Chapter 9, we are bombarded with all sorts of information about food. Some is good, but much of it is incorrect and bad. Then there are the food companies that exist to make a profit so try to sell you 'slimming foods' that will do you no good at all. It is no wonder that people are confused.

All over the media, you will read about children and adults being overweight, and fatter than we were at their age. This is true, and it is also true that it is not good to be overweight. However, this is only one side of the problem. The other side is that, more often than not, these obese children are actually undernourished.

So often the media, doctors and the public equate a good diet with obesity and losing weight, and give the impression that this is the only thing that matters. The implication is that if you are slim you are automatically healthy. This is *not* true. Obesity is important, but nutrition is about far more than this.

When I give talks, I often ask the audience to put up their hands if they think that they are undernourished. They all begin to laugh, especially the women. This is because they are bigger than they want to be or think they should be, so think that they are overfed and therefore very well nourished. However, it is easy to be overfed and undernourished, and even adults who are obese are very likely to be lacking in many nutrients. You may have seen television programmes (usually American) about extremely obese people weighing twenty stone or more. However, when tested these people are actually undernourished, in that they lack many nutrients that they need for good health. This is because junk food is high in calories, sugar and processed fat, but is lacking in vitamins, minerals, essential fatty acids and plant chemicals which help protect a myriad of diseases.

Nourishment is about nutrients, not just calories. I am just as concerned about this poor nutrition as I am about obesity. Many adults and children are lacking in important nutrients such as omega-3 fatty acids essential for the brain, zinc, magnesium and so on. Losing weight is good if you need to, other things being equal, but it is not enough to be slim. You have to be well nourished too.

The good news, however, is that fresh vegetables, fruit, meat, fish and eggs are high in nutrients and are less likely to cause obesity. If you eat the right foods in the right quantities your child can become both well nourished and – if they need to be – slimmer, although it does require some thought and effort.

In a nutshell

- Children are now being targeted by marketing companies.

- This is happening on the TV, the internet and in computer games.

- The products marketed are usually high in sugar and fat.

- This leads to obesity and children are getting fatter as time goes on.

- However obese children can also be under-nourished as fast foods are not nutritious.

- Eating the right foods means your children are well nourished as well as being a sensible weight.

Chapter 11

VEGETARIAN CHILDREN

I am often asked if vegetarian diets are better than mixed diets, and I always say that it depends on what the vegetarian eats. If we say that a vegetarian is someone who does not eat meat or fish then it is possible to be a vegetarian and live on doughnuts, pasta and pizzas, and eat very few vegetables. In fact, I have known a vegetarian who did just that. However, it is possible to have a healthy vegetarian diet, but there are certain nutrients which are more difficult to find if you do not eat meat or fish.

A vegetarian diet can be healthy, but it means thinking about what you are eating more carefully. It is easier to ingest more nutrients if you eat meat and fish. A meat eater who also has lots of vegetables has a better diet than a vegetarian who lives on cheese, wheat and Quorn. Some people become vegetarians because they feel that it is more ethical, and some because they feel that it is healthier. Either way, they need to think carefully about what they eat and make sure that their diet contains all the nutrients that they need.

Raising your children as vegetarian needs a great deal of thought and care. It is important to look at the nutritional values of foods to make sure that your child is getting enough. Doctor and nutritionist Dr Natasha Campbell-McBride argues that we have a very limited ability to digest plant foods and the stomach produces acid and pepsin, which can only digest animal protein such as meat, fish and eggs.[1] She thinks that vegetarian diets are not good for children because they can be lacking in nutrients. In many ways, it is easier to be well nourished on a mixed diet. However, if you are committed to vegetarianism, you need to make sure that your child is getting all the nutrients they need from that diet.

Children sometimes decide themselves that they want to become vegetarian for ethical reasons, usually when they are older. However, this is not a good idea unless they are prepared to learn about nutrition and understand what they may be lacking. So often children just cut out meat-based foods without having any idea what they are losing. Meats contain the highest amount of nutrients such as vitamin B1, B2, B3, B6, B12, vitamin A, vitamin D and vitamin K2. It is your job as their parent to make sure your child is aware of their nutritional needs.

Here are the key nutrients that are more difficult to get from this way of eating, and how they might be obtained:

Omega-3 fatty acids

The particular fats we are looking at here are eicosapen-
taenoic acid (EPA) and docosahexaenoic acid (DHA). In
Chapter 3 we saw just how important these are for brain
development and function throughout our whole lives. We
cannot make them in our bodies and so we need to get them
from our diet, and this is why they are called 'essential fatty
acids'. However, they come only from oily fish. You can get
omega-3 from walnuts and flaxseeds, but the fat in nuts and
seeds has to be converted to DHA in the body. This requires
other nutrients and not every individual is good at making
this conversion. However, if you are set on a vegetarian diet
eating flaxseeds or walnuts makes sense. Of course, you do
not want these important omega-3 fats to have to compete
with all the processed oils found in most shop-bought pack-
aged foods, so try to keep processed oils to the minimum.

Protein

Protein is vital for everyone. It is needed to make hormones,
enzymes, antibodies against diseases, build bones, muscles,
skin and blood, and is essential for growth and repair. Protein
is made up of certain chemicals called amino acids. A complete protein contains twenty-five amino acids, but most
vegetarian protein foods are not complete. That means that
they contain some of the amino acids, but not all. Traditional
vegetarian diets combine different foods together. For example, many Asian dishes combine chickpeas, lentils, vegetables

and yogurt together so that you get all twenty-five amino acids in the finished dish, even if not in each individual food.

Eggs contain protein, but only about 6g per egg. We need much more than that depending on age. The only vegetarian, non-animal protein foods that are quite high in protein are soya and quinoa (which is similar to couscous but more nutritious). I urge you to study food tables and work out which foods to combine so that your child gets all the protein they need in the right amounts. This is something vegetarians need to be careful about. I have seen children eating meals that contain very little protein at all. For example, pasta with a little sauce contains hardly any.

Zinc

Vegetarians can become low in zinc, as this mineral is highest in animal foods like fish and meat. Zinc is very important for children as it is involved in growth, immunity and energy production. Signs of a deficiency are a poor sense of taste and smell, stretch marks, acne or greasy skin, and a loss of appetite. Children with low zinc may have poor immunity, causing them to get infections more often, and white spots on their fingernails. All boys need extra zinc from around age twelve.

Vegetarians can get zinc from sesame seeds, Brazil nuts, whole wheat, oats, almonds, chickpeas and lentils, but if you rely on cheese and pasta you won't be getting enough. Also be aware that wheat and cereals are high in phytates, which affect the absorption of any zinc they do contain.

There are blood tests for zinc deficiency and a taste test where you drink a solution and decide what it tastes like – your answer indicates whether you are zinc deficient. Zinc can be supplemented, but it is best to get zinc from natural sources rather than supplements.

Iron

Iron is part of the haemoglobin in the blood. Its function is to transport oxygen and carbon dioxide to and from our cells. Too little can cause anaemia, pale skin, sore tongue, fatigue and listlessness. Be aware that wheat and cereal contain phytates, which can hinder absorption. The form of iron that is best absorbed is called haem iron from meat, but watercress, nuts, eggs, seeds (especially pumpkin), wheat germ, parsley, raisins and prunes are all good alternative sources of iron.

Vitamin B12

Because this is found only in animal foods, vegetarians can become deficient and vegans need to take a supplement. A deficiency can be serious and cause anaemia, but it has also been associated with other conditions. Vegetarians can get vitamin B12 from milk, yogurt and eggs. The latest research has found a connection between low levels of vitamin B12 and autism.[2]

Don't fill up on cheese

A vegetarian diet needs more thought and care to ensure that your child gets all the nutrients that they need. Because it is so important, I will repeat that you should be careful not to fill up on lots of cereals, pasta and grains, as these can take much-needed minerals out of the body. In addition, if you are vegetarian it is not a good idea to get your protein from eating too much cheese. Do your research, and find out about the nutrition content of different vegetarian foods so that you know exactly how to get all the nutrients you need.

As discussed in Chapter 9, it is not a good idea to use Quorn as a source of protein as it is a processed manufactured food. It is better to keep to fresh natural unadulterated food.

In a nutshell

- Whether or not a vegetarian diet is a good thing depends on what you eat.

- Vegetarian diets need to be thought about carefully to ensure the right intake of all important nutrients.

- If a child decides to become a vegetarian, as a parent you need to monitor their diet carefully and be aware of the nutritional content of different foods.

- Nutrients that are likely to be lacking in a vegetarian diet are: iron, zinc, vitamin B12, omega-3 fatty acids and complete proteins.

- It is not a good idea to fill up on wheat-based foods or cheese.

Chapter 12

CHILDREN'S PARTIES

Parties are a particular bone of contention for many parents. We may want to give our children a healthy diet, but when we take them to parties, we often find nothing but a sea of junk food. On the one hand we want our kids to have fun, but on the other hand we do not accept that fun has to involve eating lots of sugar, processed food, fizzy drinks, artificial flavourings and colours and so on. It's no wonder that some children get overexcited, have tantrums and start climbing the walls at parties!

Parents may also feel that when they host a party themselves other parents expect to see this type of food on offer. Your children might campaign for the same food they get at other parties. You or your children might feel that you will be seen as boring, odd or even mean if you don't offer conventional party food. But what is odd about wanting your children – and their friends – to be healthy?

Alternatively, you might feel that bad food at the odd party does not matter very much. However, as it is often the norm to invite every child in the class, many children go to *lots* of parties.

Learning to think bad food = fun

I think having bad food at parties *does* matter. Aside from the fact that these foods are not good for your children's health, 'party food' teaches children that having fun, enjoying themselves and being given treats *means* eating sweets, crisps, cakes and having fizzy drinks.

It is all about association. Children begin to associate happy feelings with these foods. This might mean that later in life they find they want these sweet foods when they feel down or are having a bad time. This is exactly what happens. Parties and fun come to mean 'party food' which means mainly sugar.

It's all about presentation

Healthy party food need not be boring. It's all about presentation, and healthy food can look as imaginative and fun as shop-bought foods.

- Don't let yourself be pressurised by other mothers. Serve what you know is right and make it look and taste delicious.

- Serve savoury foods first. If you do this, the children are more likely fill themselves up with good things and have little room for sweeter foods, if you have them.

- Serve popular 'commercial' foods, but prepare them yourself in a healthier way.

- Make the food interesting, attractive and colourful. Rather than serving large pieces of one or two foods, serve small pieces of a larger variety.

- Use colourful plates, cups, straws, etc.

The key is not to dwell on the fact or make it obvious that the children are 'not having' certain things. Just put out the food you want your children to have, and keep quiet.

Other children's parties

Going to other children's parties is more difficult. Encourage your children to eat the savoury food first, and follow it with just a little of the sweet food. If they have been eating healthily since birth, they may prefer the savoury food anyway. Another idea is to give them a large nutritious lunch before they go in the hope that they will not want to eat very much when they are there.

Boxes or buffets?

Some parents feel that a buffet is better because then children can pick what they like. However, I remember seeing one child at a party tip the whole serving plate full of the food he liked on to his own plate, waste most of it and leave none for the others. Another idea is to give each child their own box with a mixture of goodies. Of course this could also result in a large amount of waste if they don't like what's on offer. Perhaps a compromise could be their own box, with a few extra bits on the side.

Ideas for healthy party food

For younger children it is better to have a variety of very small bites so that they can pick and choose – if they don't like something there is less waste, and if they do like it they can have more of the same.

- Bite-sized sandwiches with nut butters. Cut the bread into stars or other shapes with pastry cutters.

- Very small homemade beefburgers or small meatballs (see below).

- Mini rice cakes with tomato paste and grated cheese.

- Healthy home-made mini pizzas with a very thin base and lots of topping.

- Mini yogurts.

- Pinwheel sandwiches. Cut off the crusts. Spread with butter and filling, roll up the bread and cut into slices.

- Cubes of cheese with grapes.

- Healthy knickerbocker glories. To make these, layer different coloured small pieces of fruit in plastic see-through cups. Add a dollop of yogurt or fresh cream on the top.

- Plates of colourful small fruits like berries, grapes, etc. for small hands to pick up easily.

- Make fruit smoothies and serve in small cups.

- Chicken and vegetable kebabs for older children (younger ones may poke the sticks in their eyes!).

- Fruit kebabs can also be fun for older children, with layers of different coloured fruits.

Making popular foods more healthily

There are ways of making popular foods healthier and these can be served up at parties. We should try to give our children the best food all of the time, but that means that they can't have some of their favourite and popular foods if cooked according to instructions. Many of these can be made in a healthier way. For example:

- Natural hamburgers: these can be made quite easily by shaping fresh organic mince into patties and baking in the oven.

- Meatballs: again, shaped from fresh organic mince.

- Fish fingers: cut fresh cod or haddock into finger shapes. Bake in the oven.

- Sauces for meat: buy organic tomato paste and add in

blended cooked carrots, onions, cabbage and other vegetables.

- Healthier chips: heat some coconut oil in the oven, cut potatoes into chip shapes and add them to the oil. Bake.

- Healthier pizza: buy some fresh chemical-free pizza dough and roll it out thinly, add a layer of tomato paste and lots of vegetables, salmon or sardines. You can really add what you like and what your children will eat. Shop-bought pizzas are mainly dough with hardly any topping. This makes money for the manufacturer but does little for your child.

- Chocolate dessert: mix coconut cream with cocoa to taste and add a few teaspoons of juice from an orange. This makes an acceptable chocolatey treat that children can enjoy.

- Ice-lollies: blend mixed fruit and put into lolly moulds with sticks and freeze. For a creamy dessert do the same with coconut cream (sold in small boxes in the supermarket).

- Knickerbocker glories: fill tall slim glasses with layers of fruits of various colours. A layer of fresh cream will not hurt but if you prefer you can use thick yogurt.

Party drinks

Although water is the best drink for children, I can understand parents not wanting to offer that alone at a party as it might be seen as rather boring. Diluted fruit juice is better and cheaper than individual fruit juice cartons or squash. Serve it in a colourful jug and it will be just as acceptable.

In a nutshell

- Children's parties are often a difficult time for parents who want their children to eat healthily.

- Parents should not feel pressurised by convention and other parents to give their children junk foods at these times.

- Most parties offer junk foods containing food with high sugar, processed fats and all manner of artificial additives.

- This is bad because children learn to associate sweet and junk food with fun, treats and having a good time.

- It is possible to produce healthier party foods that are both attractive and delicious.

- Diluted fruit juice is healthier and much nicer than squashes or fizzy pop.

- Popular foods like hamburgers are nutritious if home-made from minced meat.

Chapter 13

LEARNING DIFFICULTIES

Learning difficulties appear to have skyrocketed in the last few years. Some argue that they were always there but were not being diagnosed. That may account for some cases, but most experts agree that there is a real increase in conditions such as dyslexia, dyspraxia, attention deficit disorder (ADD), attention deficit disorder with hyperactivity (ADHD) and autism. However, we must be careful about giving children labels and realise that there is still much controversy about what these labels actually mean.

Director of the charity Food and Behaviour Research, Dr Alex Richardson, argues that 'in milder forms . . . it is a matter of opinion (and considerable controversy) where the dividing lines should be drawn'.[1] However, she does make the point that what we eat is vitally important for the brain as well as every other aspect of our health. She argues that, 'Food and diet are important to all of us . . . because without the right nutrients it simply isn't possible for our brains and bodies to develop properly and to function properly.'

Therefore, for all children these are vitally important, but even more so if a child has one of these conditions.

Dyslexia and dyspraxia

If your child has been diagnosed with dyslexia or dyspraxia there is much that you can do on the nutritional side (although nutrition is not the only way that you should try to help your child). A good natural diet such as that recommended in this book is very important for children with these problems. There are books which specialise in this area, including *They Are What You Feed Them* by Dr Alex Richardson.

Attention deficit disorder (ADD) and attention deficit hyperactivity disorder (ADHD)

These are some of the most common behavioural disorders in children. Children with these conditions may have the following problems: they find it hard to pay attention, they act on impulse and they are hyperactive. They have difficulty organising tasks, make careless mistakes, are easily distracted and talk or chatter all the time. Around 5 per cent of children in the UK and far more in the USA are thought to have ADHD. This does not seem very many until we realise that this amounts to 367,000 UK children, a very large number. Some doctors have argued that ADHD relates to the lack of the neurotransmitter dopamine in the brain.

Good food is vitally important for these children. A study published in the *European Journal of Clinical Nutrition* looked at 4,000 children aged four-and-a-half to seven and found that children eating a diet high in junk food in early childhood were associated with increased hyperactivity later on.[2] In the study 'junk food' referred to burgers, coated poultry, crisps and chocolate.

Nutrition for children with learning difficulties

A good diet is extremely important for all children, but for those with learning difficulties it is even more important. The main things that need to be considered from a nutritional point of view are:

- Balancing blood sugar
- Checking for food intolerances
- Increasing omega-3 fatty acids
- Eating the best natural diet

Balancing blood sugar

Return to Chapter 4, where I discuss how to keep your child's blood sugar stable, avoiding the highs and lows.

Food intolerances

There have been many studies to try to find out which

foods, if any, contribute to ADHD. The foods that can affect behaviour are wheat, corn, yeast, soya, peanuts and eggs. No children should have artificial colours, flavours or other chemical additives, but this is even more important when considering children with learning difficulties.

Increasing omega-3 fats

We discussed in Chapter 3 the importance of omega-3 fats for everyone, including children. This is even more important for children with these problems. Research has shown that many children with ADHD are low in these nutrients. A study published in the journal *Neuropharmacology* showed that supplementation with omega-3 fatty acids reduced symptoms of ADHD more than when compared to a placebo.[3] It improved the children's attention as rated by parents.

Omega-3 is lacking in most children's diets (as well as the diets of adults), and the processed fats we eat today take the place of or compete with any omega-3 we do get.

Many studies relate to supplementing omega-3 in pill form, but omega-3 occurs naturally in oily fish, so why not simply give children fish with all its associated nutrients and co-factors?

It is not possible for a little capsule of fish oil to compete with tablespoons of vegetable oil, margarine or cake that are full of it. If you are a home baker, you will know just how much margarine or butter is needed to make a cake. It is a huge amount! Therefore, as well as giving your child oily fish or supplements, you also need to keep these unhealthy processed fats and oils out of their diet.

Minerals like zinc

Zinc is very important as it performs many functions in the body. For example, it is needed for more than two hundred different reactions in the body and brain. It is vital for growth, and a deficiency has been associated with poor immunity leading to infections, hyperactivity, autism, anorexia and learning difficulties. Children who are low in zinc can have a poor sense of taste or smell (leading them to crave highly flavoured, salted or sugary foods), fatigue and stunted growth. They can have white spots on their fingernails. Dr Alex Richardson makes the point that zinc is needed to be able to utilise omega-3 and omega-6 fatty acids, and according to her, a deficiency could lead to a brain that does not function properly.[4]

Zinc is the mineral that children are most likely to be deficient in. The average intake in the UK is about half the recommended amount. Boys may need extra zinc from the age of about twelve. The richest source of zinc is oysters, but other fish and meat are good sources, as well as nuts, seeds and the germ of grains. As mentioned in Chapter 11, vegetarians can become low in zinc because the highest amounts are contained in foods originating from animals.

Food additives

Many chemicals are added to foods in the modern diet. This is something relatively new; we did not have them even as recently as a hundred years ago. They include artificial colourings, flavourings and preservatives. Not all are bad. For example, E300, an antioxidant which stops food going rancid, is actually vitamin C. However, many are not good for children and I advise you to avoid them as much as possible.

In December 2009, the British government asked food manufacturers to remove most artificial food dyes from their products and I would recommend that no children have these. However, it is even more important for children with any learning disorder. Some studies have shown that children with ADHD improve on a diet free of artificial colourings. We do not really know what these additives are doing to us, so why have them? If you are eating the diet that I recommend you should avoid most of them anyway.

In a nutshell

- Learning difficulties appear to be on the increase.

- The best food is vitally important for good brain development and the ability to learn.

- The diet needs to be able to keep blood sugar balanced and have good levels of omega-3 fatty acids, vitamins and trace minerals.

- Parents should also get their children checked for food intolerances and nutritional deficiencies such as zinc.

- A good natural diet should be served without food additives.

Chapter 14

OLDER CHILDREN

If you start feeding your children the best nutritious foods when they are young, they will hopefully grow into happy and healthy adolescents. But then, suddenly, your teenager wants to eat something different. They might decide not to eat certain foods at all. They might want to become a vegetarian, or crave lots of junk foods. Or worse still they may decide to go on a slimming diet and eat very little at all.

Becoming adolescents

This can be a very difficult time for parents who just want the best for their children. Because of hormonal shifts and other changes, such as going to a new school, adolescence is for some a time of self-doubt, emotional upheaval and even depression. Teenagers become concerned about their image and appearance, and this matters hugely at this time. As a parent, you will be concerned about their ability to focus at school as the workload intensifies. You'll want to see them as healthy and happy as they can be, while they go through these hormonal changes and emotional imbalances.

Sadly, a national diet survey found that British teenagers ate more fast food, sweets and chocolate than any other age group.[1] Of course, as discussed in Chapter 10, this isn't helped by the food industry's marketing practices, and most adolescents will also want to do what their peers do.

Good nutrition helps

Eating well in adolescence is extremely important, because the right diet can help protect your child from many woes, both physical and mental. A study published in the *American Journal of Public Health* looked at the relationship between diet and mental health in children and adolescents.[2] This was a review of twelve epidemiological studies (comparing different societies), which found that there was a significant relationship between poor diet and mental health.

The description 'poor diet' referred to one that was higher in saturated fat, sugar and processed foods, and the good diet was one which was high in vegetables, salads, fruit and fish. The study concluded that a high sugar diet can affect proteins in the brain and is related to inflammation.

The brain is not separate from the body. Neurotransmitters are made from nutrients such as protein and B vitamins, omega-3, etc. Therefore, it is extra important that children be well fed at this time both for their physical and mental wellbeing. A good diet helps with all aspects of growth and development: emotional, intellectual and physical.

Making their own choices

One problem is that adolescence is a time when children are out of the home and unaccompanied for much of the day. They can make their own choices about food, and they have their own money. And they are certainly targeted by aggressive marketers and food producers. The best way to keep your teenager well fed is to feed them good food from a young age and to teach them about nutrition. However, if you have come to this book with your children already teenagers, how can you encourage them to choose healthier food?

In my experience as a nutritionist, there is no point in telling children or teenagers that good nutrition will prevent them having a heart attack or type 2 diabetes in later life. 'Later life' is a very long way away from their point of view. You need to tune into what they really want now. Adolescents are very self-critical, and many are also very influenced by film stars, the media and their peers. While this can be a bad thing, you can turn it to your advantage by explaining, truthfully, how eating well can give them what they want.

Good food means looking better

For adolescents, appearance is very important. They want to look great. Eating the best food can largely give them this. Because everything we are comes from food (plus, of course, water and air), good food will give them the clearest skin, the brightest eyes, the strongest nails, the shiniest hair and the most attractive figure or physique. If they don't eat well they will be more prone to acne, greasy hair and excess weight. Boys in particular are prone to having spots at this age, so impress upon them that eating the right food can help. Acne can be caused by a deficiency of zinc, but because of all the other nutrients to be gained, I recommend they eat zinc-rich foods rather than take supplements.

All nutrients are needed for good looks. For instance, a lack of omega-3 and/or omega-6 can cause dry hair, dandruff, dry skin, eczema and dry eyes. Low zinc can lead to greasy skin and acne. A lack of protein can result in poor quality hair, nails and low mood. These are just a few simple examples, but the diet recommended in this book should improve all of these things.

But be careful

When telling your child that good nutrition means better looks, it is important that they don't start thinking that they should be stick thin. They should realise that having an attractive figure does not mean being skeletal, and that there is no place in healthy eating for starvation or strange diets. Sometimes teenagers confuse healthy eating with eating very little at all or with eating strange and odd things. You will have to watch for this.

Be careful about telling a child that they are overweight. Anorexia and other eating disorders are a big worry for many parents today. It is also not a good idea for mothers, in particular, to talk about how they themselves need to lose weight and to relate being thin to being beautiful or successful. Although obesity is a problem in the West, children should not expect to look like today's fashion models, who are abnormally thin and far too emaciated for good health. I cannot stress this enough: it is simply not the case that being very thin equates with good health.

Eating well involves good wholesome natural foods, the kind of foods that are easy to make and taste delicious. Not eating well or enough can lead to dry skin and hair, broken nails, low energy and low moods. Impress upon your teenager that health and attractiveness go together, and health comes from what you eat.

If your teenager likes a particular food this can be adapted to make it as nutritious as possible.

Good food means achieving more

Teenagers who play sports should be told that the best diet will help them do better, have more energy and improved muscle tone. Athletes are usually very interested in nutrition and careful about what they eat.

If your child loves to study and wants to do well at school, you can say that good nutrition is important to brain function such as concentration.

Becoming a student and leaving home

If you teach your children about healthy eating long before they leave home for university or college, it will be easier for them to cope better when they get there. They will be in better shape both physically and mentally, and will be less likely to become depressed. Emotional difficulties can be a problem for new students, as they find their way in a new environment with greater pressures. The right food affects mood, sleep, concentration, energy and just about everything else. Every child should learn about what to eat from a young age, and as they get older how to buy the best food and cook it. Of course, it goes without saying that they should also be advised about the dangers of alcohol!

Every adolescent should learn some simple recipes before they leave for university or college or for work and a flat-share. Students and those just starting out in the world of work won't have very much spare cash, so they need to know which foods are cheap and easy to prepare, as well as being nutritious. On the other hand, because what they eat is so important, they should be advised against skimping on food so that they can use the money elsewhere. Good nutrition will enable them to learn more, work better and have more fun in both the short and long term.

In a nutshell

- Adolescents should know that the right food will help them look and perform the best.

- They should learn about nutrition from a young age.

- Students should be taught to cook nutritious food before going away to university or college.

Chapter 15

OUR CHEMICALISED WORLD

Although eating the right food is extremely important, it is not the only thing that matters as far as your child's health is concerned. The environment that they live in is also significant. The problem is that we live in a toxic world. Every year new chemicals are being introduced into the environment and into our bodies. They are present in the food we eat, the liquids we drink and the air we breathe. They are in the home, in shopping centres, in schools and even in hospitals. They affect us as adults, but can affect children even more because their bodies are so much smaller. We cannot know how much they affect us or our children and we certainly do not know how combinations of them affect our health and wellbeing.

Free chemicals

Manufacturers go to a great deal of effort to encourage us to use their toiletries and cosmetics, and we fall for it. Some of us have mountains of personal care products in our bathrooms, but they can be full of new and potentially toxic chemicals. Chemicals can be absorbed through the skin and affect our bodies. They are relatively new to our lives, and we do not really know what combinations of them are doing to us. Mothers coming home from hospital with new babies are often given free bags of sample products such as shampoos, bubble baths and baby lotions. The implication is that these products are what children need, but they are usually full of substances that your child is fine without – the only personal care products a child needs are natural toothpaste, plus toxin-free soap and shampoo.

As parents, I believe it is our responsibility to protect our children as much as possible from new chemicalised products, but it is not always easy. We cannot do very much about schools and hospitals, but we can have an effect on our own environment at home. Again, we can try our best. Non-toxic products can be bought in health food shops, on the internet, and even in some supermarkets.

In the bathroom

Many people think that these products must be safe because they are allowed to be sold. However, how much do we really know about them and the effect of combining different products? If you read the list of ingredients you will see that they are full of chemicals. These can be absorbed into the skin very well.

Bubble baths

While a bath full of bubbles can be fun, it is not worth the possible danger. Your child will soak in this product for quite a long time while in the bath, and it will remain on your child's skin after bathing. Our skin is not a very good barrier and can absorb some chemicals very well. Let your child have fun with boats or ducks rather than toxic chemicals.

Talc or talcum powder

This is not needed and just adds more chemicals into your child's life. It is suspected that using talcum powder in the lower regions can cause ovarian cancer in adults.

Shampoos and conditioners

Shampoos, soaps and toothpaste usually contain the chemical sodium lauryl (laureth) sulphate, which is very toxic. They might also contain paraben compounds, which have been known to interfere with hormones. Fortunately, it is possible to buy better shampoos that do not contain these chemicals.

Moisturisers

These are not needed. They are full of chemicals and you should avoid them. Your child's skin should not be so dry that they need to have these extra oils. If you give them the correct oils in their food, and forego all processed oils and fats, their skin should be fine. In cases where there is an illness that requires more moisturising, ask your GP to recommend something. Some natural products can be used on the skin itself. For example, dry skin on the heels can be helped with pure coconut oil.

Baby wipes

Water is cheaper and just as good for cleaning a baby's bottom. Do not use other wipes on a baby's face. Extra chemicals are not needed and plain water is better.

In the kitchen

Cooking utensils

Use stainless steel pots rather than Teflon coated or those made from aluminium.

Detergents

These stay on the clothes which is not good, especially on items that are next to the skin like vests. Try to use natural products as much as possible.

Cleaning products

Cleaning products are many and varied. There is a vast

amount of these in the shops and we are given the impression that our homes cannot be hygienic without them. This is not true. Most are not needed and many contain chemicals that children are better off without. Ordinary natural substances like lemon juice and vinegar are very good for cleaning baths and bathroom equipment. Plain water is fine for windows and washing down paintwork. We do not need all these sprays that stay in the atmosphere long after they have been used.

Plastics

We live in a plasticised world. Everywhere we look there are products made from all different forms of plastic from wallpapers to toys, baby bottles, children's dishes, mattresses and so on. Children tend to be more exposed to these for reasons of safety, and to avoid the risk of breakages. The problem is that plastics can leach out a chemical called bisphenol A (BPA), which can cause hormonal cancers. If you buy bottled water, try to get it in glass bottles. Don't cook food in plastic containers or use cling film on food.

Ventilation

Keep your home well ventilated by opening windows regularly. Buy houseplants, which clean the air by consuming toxic gasses and replacing them with oxygen.

Pesticides

Do not use these in your home or garden. Talk to your neighbours about the dangers from these chemicals, and ask them not to use them either.

New goods

These too can contain toxic chemicals, but you can reduce your toxic load by being careful about them. New carpets, paints, curtains, furniture and other home decorative products can release toxic chemicals for years. If you are decorating your child's bedroom, use non-toxic paints which are available on the internet, and air the room thoroughly while your child is not in it. If you are having a new baby, perhaps put him or her into another room for a while until the newly decorated room outgases any toxic chemicals. Pregnant women need to be careful about this too.

If you can, put new goods like suitcases in the open air to release any chemicals before use. Air thoroughly any clothes that have been dry-cleaned. New cars should be thoroughly ventilated before use, or buy a car that is a year old instead. That new car smell that is liked by so many is really chemicals releasing from the plastics and other fabrics used in the vehicle's manufacture.

Out and about

Swimming is a healthy form of exercise but be careful about the pool. A study published in the *Irish Medical Journal* found that the greater the length of time that a group of boys had attended an indoor, chlorinated pool, the greater the likelihood of wheezing or having asthma.[1] However, even if your child is not obviously affected by the chlorine it is important to have a thorough wash in the shower afterwards. It is better to use pools that are disinfected with ozone.

If you are walking with children in prams or pushchairs, try to keep away from main roads where passing cars pollute the atmosphere with exhaust fumes. You often see joggers running by the side of very busy roads, and this is similarly not a good idea if your children take up running when they're older. Stick to the quieter areas or use the parks, which are more pleasant anyway.

I am not trying to scare you in discussing these products. My aim is to show that they are not needed, and for that for many, such as shampoo, there are natural equivalents. As children are smaller than adults they are more at risk from artificial chemicals in the environment.

In a nutshell

- We live in a chemicalised world. Every year more existing and new chemicals are added to our environment.

- Try to limit the amount of personal care products you use on your children, as they are more vulnerable to the chemicals in them than adults.

- The only products children need are natural soap, shampoo and toothpaste.

- Try also to use natural cleaning products, which can be bought in health food shops or online. Lemon juice and vinegar are good alternatives.

- Cook with stainless steel rather than Teflon or aluminium.

- Air new goods and dry-cleaned products as much as possible.

- If out and about on foot, keep away from main roads.

Chapter 16

TOP TIPS FOR HEALTHY EATING

- Your child's diet should consist of fresh unprocessed foods in as natural a state as possible, with nothing added or taken away. These foods contain the highest concentration of nutrients.

- The main ingredients in your child's diet should be vegetables, fruit, organic meat and chicken, fresh fish, eggs, nuts and seeds, beans, lentils, better quality grains like millet, quinoa and yogurt.

- Children need to keep their blood sugar stable with a good breakfast of protein, carbohydrate and fat.

- Stabilise blood sugar throughout the whole day with all meals and snacks based on the principle of protein, carbohydrate and fat.

- Include oily fish at least twice a week, in order to add

omega-3 fatty acids to the diet (along with protein and other important nutrients).

- Omega-6 fats can be got from eating sunflower and pumpkin seeds, as well as nuts.

- Your child should eat a rainbow of coloured fruits and vegetables every day. These contain thousands of plant or phytochemicals, which have multiple important functions within the body, helping to prevent many diseases like heart disease and cancer.

- Supplement your child's diet with vitamin D3.

- Try not to give your children sugary foods or foods with added table sugar, such as biscuits and cakes, or other food with sugar added.

- Aim to cut out or dramatically reduce the amount of vegetable oils you give your child. The only vegetable oils that can be used are good quality extra virgin olive oil and coconut fat.

- Do not give them margarine or other spreads except butter. This includes all foods made with margarine, such as cakes. Read labels carefully.

- Try to keep away from food with artificial additives such as colours, flavourings, etc.

- It is better to use organic food as much as possible.

- Cut out all fizzy and soft drinks. Use filtered water, broths or diluted fresh fruit juices instead.

- Try to keep their environment free from artificial chemicals as much as possible.

- Keep your home well ventilated and use plants to clean the air.

Chapter 17

FREQUENTLY ASKED QUESTIONS

Q. If nutrition is so important why are junk foods allowed to be sold?

A. The law states that food has to be safe; it doesn't say it has to be healthy. The difference is that there must not be mould, dirt or bacteria in food, as that will make you ill soon after you eat it. However, food does not need to be healthy and the wrong food can make you overweight or ill in the long run.

Q. If oily fish is good what about smoked salmon?

A. This is indeed an oily fish, but I would not give it to children until they are about twelve. It is smoked, which increases free radicals, and it is also very high in sodium or salt. Sodium and potassium need to be in balance with each other, so if given occasionally make sure that you include some potassium-rich foods with it. This could be cucumber, other vegetables or fruit. However, I think it is better not to give children smoked salmon or smoked mackerel.

Q. Is cod liver oil a good source of omega-3?

A. No. Cod liver oil is a source of vitamins A and D, but it is not high in omega-3. Many people are confused about this and so take cod liver oil for the wrong reasons. It used to be given to children free because of its vitamin D content in order to prevent the bone deformity rickets. However, cod is not an oily fish and you cannot take very much, because high levels can be toxic. If you need to take a fish supplement, buy one that says fish oil or salmon oil. If you need vitamin D, take a specific vitamin D supplement.

Q. It seems to be quite a lot of bother to change my child's diet.

A. It might be so at first, but after a while it becomes second nature, especially if both parents eat the same way. It will help both parents and children keep healthy in the present and in years to come.

Q. Can't children have some sweets as treats?

A. It is better to bring up your children to think of good foods, rather than shop-bought sweets, as special. If you do this, you might then find that they are not interested in sweets and prefer fruit instead. The odd sweet does not matter, but they should not be encouraged to think that sweets are a treat.

Q. Why don't doctors tell us about nutrition if it is so important?

A. Most doctors deal with people who are already sick. They have a great deal of knowledge about illnesses, but are not necessarily taught very much about nutrition at university, which takes many more years of study. Generally, most doctors would agree that good food is important and will tell you to eat fruit and vegetables, but they may not know about the detail. This is a pity because food and nutrition are implicated in many diseases.

Q. If sugar is natural, why is it so bad for us?

A. It is bad because we have managed to extract it from sugar beet and sugar cane. When extracted, the nutrients and fibre of the original plant are left behind, and the resulting product is very concentrated and devoid of nutrients.

Q. Surely a little junk food doesn't hurt?

A. It probably varies from person to person, but we just don't know how much junk food we can eat without doing harm. However, I feel that we should do our utmost to get the best food into our children most of the time. After all, very young children have few strong ideas about food and so we need to take the opportunity to influence them then. After a time, it becomes second nature.

Q. Why should we have to dilute fresh fruit juice? Surely it is a completely natural food.

A. That is true – but think how many oranges you need to make a glassful. This means you are left with a concentrate of the sugar, which is contained in the juice. It is better to eat the whole fruit with the fibre intact, and if serving juice make sure it is diluted.

Q. You have not mentioned soya. Why is that?

A. Soya is controversial. Much of it is genetically modified, and it is not clear whether this is good for us or not. I decided to include only foods that we are most sure about. Anyway, in the West it is not eaten very often.

Q. My child does not like some of the healthy foods you mention. What should I do?

A. It depends on the food. Some are more important than others. For example, if your child does not like peas, then there is no need to eat them. Other vegetables will do instead. However, if your child will not eat oily fish you will need to find another way of getting omega-3. This could be from flaxseeds or walnuts.

Q. Why can't we just eat without worrying about getting enough nutrients?

A. In the natural state we probably could, but then we just

ate what was around us. It was not processed in any way. However, nowadays food is grown differently, is then highly processed and is often stripped of many nutrients. As a result, it is not easy to be well nourished so we need to think more about what we are eating.

Q. In our family we eat anything we like, which includes junk food, but none of us is overweight. Is this OK?

A. Weight is not the only indicator of poor health. You can be slim and unhealthy. It is just as important to be well nourished as it is to be slim. We need to eat the right nutrients every day in order to feed both our brains and bodies.

Q. I know of families who seem to live on rubbish but the children seem fit and healthy.

A. It is true that this can happen, and it is also true that some people who eat healthily still become ill. However, these are just specific cases. If we look at thousands of children and adults we find that, overall, those who eat better do better.

Q. I do not want my children to become neurotic about healthy eating. Could this happen?

A. I agree. I do not want your children to become like this, and I don't want you to become neurotic either. The way to avoid this is to just give them the food you want them to eat, eat it yourself and say very little about it. Just act as if this is what you eat in your family. After all children from all over the world eat their national diet and accept it. If they do not like a particular food leave it out for a while and try introducing it later.

As they start to enjoy good foods you can start to tell them about the benefits, so by the time they leave home they have all the nutritional information they need. Cooking together helps.

Q. But isn't it easier to give my children fast food?

A. Not necessarily, as there are plenty of healthy foods that are just as quick and easy to prepare or need almost no preparation at all. These include scrambled eggs, avocados, fruit, nuts, salads, baked potatoes, tinned fish, baked salmon, etc.

Q. We are often told that red meat is not good for us. Is this true?

A. Processed meat like spam, sausages and bacon is certainly not good for us, but fresh organic meat is very different. It is very high in nutrients like B vitamins, minerals, protein, zinc and iron. We have been eating it throughout our history. However, we need to be careful how we cook it. Burnt or browned meat can contain cancer-causing chemicals, so slow cooking in stews and casseroles is better.

Q. What about cost? Is this way of eating expensive?

A. Some good foods are more expensive than cheap foods, but if you are cutting out all the junk and processed foods you will save money there. Fresh vegetables are not usually expensive and making large pots of soup with bones from the butcher can be very economical.

Q. I never learned to cook. How can I give my children healthy food?

A. You should not be afraid of cooking or need to use fancy recipes. Most dishes are easy to make, for example, baked potatoes, scrambled eggs, boiled vegetables, broths and fish done in the oven (see Chapters 5 and 6 for more examples). Start with a few simple dishes and work up from there. Never feel that you are being judged on your cooking. It is not a competition. In my opinion, simply cooked food is just as nice as a more elaborate dish.

REFERENCES

Chapter 1: Food and your child

1. Richardson, A.J., et al. (2012), 'Docosahexaenoic acid for reading, cognition and behavior in children aged 7–9 years: a randomized, controlled trial (the DOLAB Study)', *PLoS ONE*, 7, 9: e43909

Chapter 2: General aims for feeding your child

1. [No authors listed] (2009), 'Artificial Food Colouring and Hyperactivity Symptoms in Children', *Prescrire International*, 18, 103: 215

Chapter 3: The right fats

1. Montgomery, P., et al. (2013), 'Low Blood Long Chain Omega-3 Fatty Acids in UK Children Are Associated with Poor Cognitive Performance and Behavior: A Cross-Sectional Analysis from the DOLAB Study', *PLoS ONE*, 8, 6: e66697

Chapter 5: Very easy quick natural foods

1. Comerford, K.B., et al. (2016), 'The Role of Avocados in Complementary and Transitional Feeding', *Nutrients*, 8, 5: 31316

2. Kamihiro, S., et al. (2015), 'Meat quality and health implications of organic and conventional beef production', *Meat Science*, 100: 306–18

3. Crinnion, W.J., et al. (2010), 'Organic foods contain higher levels of certain nutrients, lower levels of pesticides, and may provide health benefits for the consumer', *Alternative Medical Review*, 15, 1: 4–12

Chapter 6: A day's healthy eating

1. Cooper, S.B., et al. (2011), 'Breakfast consumption and cognitive function in adolescent children', *Physiology & Behaviour*, 103, 5: 431–9

2. Liu, J., et al. (2013), 'Regular breakfast consumption is associated with increased IQ in kindergarten children', *Journal of Early Human Development*, 89, 4: 257–62

3. Evans, C.E., et al. (2010), 'A cross-sectional survey of children's packed lunches in the UK: food-and nutrient-based results', *Journal of Epidemiology and Community Health*, 64, 11: 977–83

4. Farris, A.R., et al. (2014), 'Nutritional comparison of packed and school lunches in pre-kindergarten and kindergarten children following the implementation of the 2012–2013 National School Lunch Program standards', *Journal of Nutritional Education and Behaviour*, 46, 6: 621–6

Chapter 7: Vitamin D

1. Andiran, N., et al. (2012), 'Vitamin D deficiency in children and adolescents', *Journal of Pediatric Endocrinology*, 4: 25–69

2. https://www.gov.uk/government/publications/vitamin-d-advice-on-supplements-for-at-risk-groups

3. Akkermans, M.D., et al. (2016), 'Iron and Vitamin D Deficiency in Healthy Young Children in Western Europe Despite Current Nutritional Recommendations', *Journal of Paediatric Gastroenterology Nutrition*, 62, 4: 635–42

Chapter 8: What not to feed your children

1. World Cancer Research Fund/American Institute for Cancer Research (2007), *Second Expert Report: Food, Nutrition, Physical activity and the Prevention of Cancer: a Global Perspective* (Washington DC: AIRC)

2. Marrero, N.M., et al. (2014), 'Salt intake of children and adolescents in South London: consumption levels and dietary sources', *Hypertension*, 63: 1026–32

3. Delmis, J. (2010), 'Effect of diet and salt intake on the development of hypertension in children and adolescents', *Acta Medica Croatica*, 64, 2: 111–14

4. He, F.J., et al. (2008), 'Salt and blood pressure in children and adolescents', *Journal of Human Hypertension*, 22: 4–11

5. Campbell-McBride, N. (2010), *Gut and Psychology Syndrome: Natural Treatment for Autism, ADD/ADHD, Dyslexia, Dyspraxia, Depression, Schizophrenia* (London: Medinform Publishing)

5. Avena, N.M., et al. (2008), 'Evidence for sugar addiction: Behavioral and neurochemical effects of intermittent, excessive sugar intake', *Neuroscience & Behavioral Reviews*, 32, 1: 20–39

Chapter 9: Foods sold as 'heathy' that are not

1. Schwartz, M.B., et al. (2008), 'Examining the nutritional quality of breakfast cereals marketed to children', *Journal of the American Dietetic Association*, 108, 4: 702–5

2. Imamura, F., et al. (2015), 'Consumption of sugar sweetened beverages, artificially sweetened beverages, and fruit juice and incidence of type 2 diabetes: systematic review, meta-analysis, and estimation of population attributable fraction', *British Medical Journal*, 351: h3576

3. Williams, D. (2015), *Wheat Belly* (London: Harper Thorsons)

4. Richardson, A. (2006), *They Are What You Feed Them* (London: Thorsons)

   [The researcher Dr Alex Richardson has said that the UK still allows some artificial additives that are banned in other EU countries.]

5. Lau, K., et al. (2006), 'Synergistic interactions between commonly used food additives in a developmental neurotoxicity test', *Toxicology Sciences*, 90, 1: 178–87

    [A study at Liverpool University looked at four additives: monosodium glutamate, the colours quinoline yellow and brilliant blue, and aspartame.]

6. Bateman, B., et al. (2004), 'The effects of a double blind, placebo controlled, artificial food colourings and benzoate preservative challenge on hyperactivity in a general population sample of preschool children', *Archives of Disease in Childhood*, 89, 6: 506–511

    [In a study conducted in the Isle of Wight, researchers from the University of Southampton looked at the effect of certain artificial colourings on children's behaviour.]

Chapter 10: Marketing food for children

1. Cheyne, A.D., et al. (2013), 'Marketing sugary cereals to children in the digital age: a content analysis of 17 child-targeted websites', *Journal of Health Communication*, 18, 5: 563–82

2. Boyland, E.J. and Whalen, R. (2015), 'Food advertising to children and its effects on diet: review of recent prevalence and impact data', *Pediatric Diabetes*, 16, 5: 331–7

3. Mehta, K., et al. (2012), 'Marketing foods to children through product packaging: prolific, unhealthy and misleading', *Public Health Nutrition*, 15, 9: 1763–70

4. Kelly, B., et al. (2008), 'Internet food marketing on popular children's websites and food product websites in Australia', *Public Health Nutrition*, 11, 11: 118–7

5. Lobstein, T., et al. (2015), 'Child and adolescent obesity: part of a bigger picture', *The Lancet*, 385, 9986: 2510–20

Chapter 11: Vegetarian children

1. Campbell-McBride, N. (2010), *Gut and Psychology Syndrome: Natural Treatment for Autism, ADD/ADHD, Dyslexia, Dyspraxia, Depression, Schizophrenia* (London: Medinform Publishing)

References

2. Wang, T., et al. (2016), 'Serum concentration of 25-hydroxyvitamin D in autism spectrum disorder: a systematic review and meta-analysis', *European Child and Adolescent Psychiatry*, 25, 4: 341–50

Chapter 13: Learning difficulties

1. Richardson, A. (2006), *They Are What You Feed Them* (London: Thorsons)

2. Wiles, N.J., et al. (2009), '"Junk food" diet and childhood behavioural problems: Results from the ALSPAC cohort', *European Journal of Clinical Nutrition*, 63, 4: 491–8

3. Luchtman, D.W. and Song, C. (2013), 'Cognitive enhancement by omega-3 fatty acids from child-hood to old age: findings from animal and clinical studies', *Neuropharmacology*, Jan, 64: 550–65

4. Richardson, A. (2006), *They Are What You Feed Them* (London: Thorsons)

Chapter 14: Older children

1. Board of Science and Education, British Medical Association (2003), *Adolescent Health* (London: British Medical Association)

   [Sadly, a national diet survey found that British teenagers ate more fast food, sweets and chocolate than any other group.]

2. O'Neil. A., et al. (2014), 'Relationship between diet and mental health in children and adolescents: a systematic review', *American Journal of Public Health*, 104, 10: e31–42.

Chapter 15: Our chemicalised world

1. Cotter, A., et al. (2009), 'The pool chlorine hypothesis and asthma among boys', *Irish Medical Journal*, 102, 3: 79–82

INDEX

Index